HOW TO FIX YOUR BICYCLE

SEVENTH EDITION

by HELEN GARVY

illustrated by T WHITE

SHIRE PRESS

Cover and section drawings by Dan Bessie

Library of Congress Card Number: 93-83446
ISBN: 0-918828-11-2

SHIRE PRESS
26873 Hester Creek Road
Los Gatos, CA 95030
(408) 353-4253

CONTENTS

BASICS

ADJUSTMENTS AND OVERHAUL

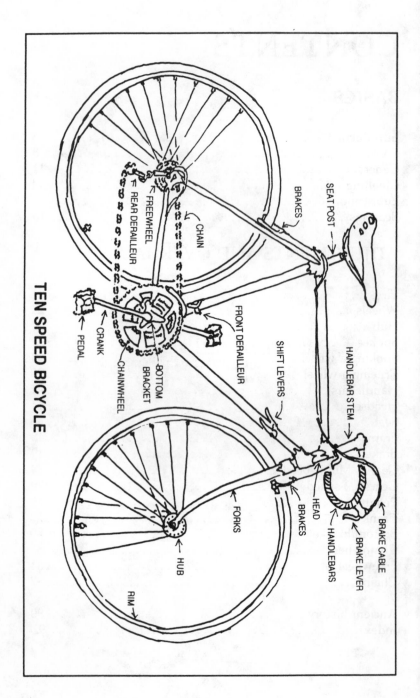

TEN SPEED BICYCLE

FREEWHEEL

REAR DERAILLEUR

CHAIN

BRAKES

SEAT POST

PEDAL

CRANK

CHAINWHEEL

BOTTOM BRACKET

FRONT DERAILLEUR

SHIFT LEVERS

HANDLEBAR STEM

FORKS

BRAKES

HEAD

HANDLEBARS

BRAKE LEVER

BRAKE CABLE

HUB

RIM

2

BASICS

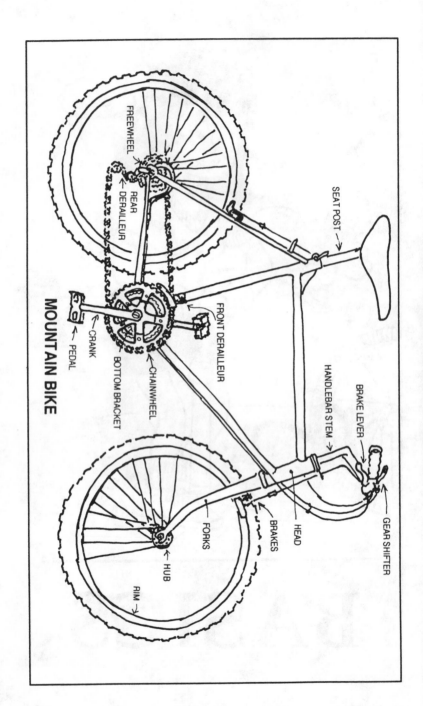

MOUNTAIN BIKE

FREEWHEEL

REAR DERAILLEUR

SEAT POST

CRANK

PEDAL

BOTTOM BRACKET

CHAINWHEEL

FRONT DERAILLEUR

HANDLEBAR STEM

BRAKE LEVER

GEAR SHIFTER

FORKS

BRAKES

HEAD

HUB

RIM

INTRODUCTION

This is a book to help you fix your bicycle. Bikes are basically simple machines and you should be able to fix most things that go wrong with your bike. I had bikes since I was a little kid and I always understood that since it was my bicycle, it was also my responsibility to take care of it. I tried to keep my bike out of the rain, clean, well oiled, and adjusted. When things broke I fixed them myself — no one else in my family offered to do it and my allowance was too small to allow me to take it to a bike shop. No one ever told me I couldn't fix things myself — so I just tried and discovered I could.

This book is to encourage you to try. I'll explain how things work as well as what nut to turn because I think that if you understand how things work, and why, you'll have an easier time finding and fixing specific things that go wrong. If you already understand basic mechanical principals — a bike is just a simple machine. If you're not familiar with machines — here's your chance to learn.

There are three main things to remember when working on your bike:

1) **GO EASY** and think about what you are doing. If you take something apart, make sure to notice what it looked like before. Draw yourself a diagram if necessary. Read the section on GENERAL TIPS (p. 11) carefully.

2) **USE COMMON SENSE.** If something goes wrong, look carefully. Figure out how the thing is supposed to work. Think. Where could something go wrong? Try something and see if that works. If it doesn't, try something else.

3) **DON'T BE AFRAID OF YOUR BIKE.** You should be able to take most of it apart and put it back together correctly, especially if you are neat and careful and watch what you are doing. Don't be careless, but don't be afraid.

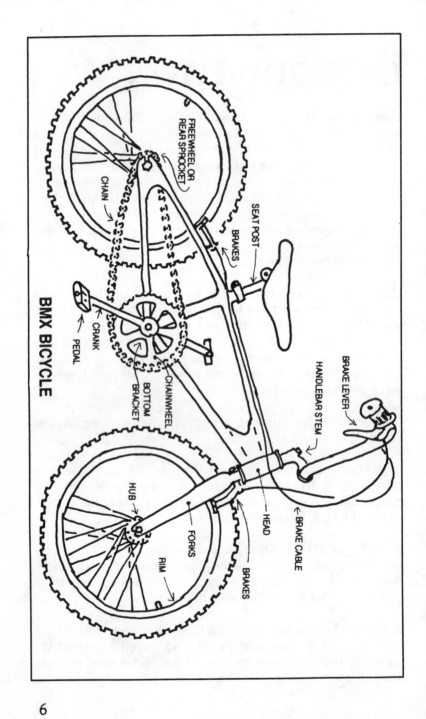

BMX BICYCLE

FREEWHEEL OR REAR SPROCKET

CHAIN

SEAT POST

BRAKES

CRANK

PEDAL

CHAINWHEEL

BOTTOM BRACKET

BRAKE LEVER

HANDLEBAR STEM

HUB

FORKS

RIM

HEAD

BRAKE CABLE

BRAKES

HOW TO USE THIS BOOK. To save space I've tried to repeat things as little as possible. Because of this and because many mechanical principles apply to more that one part of the bike, you should read through the book quickly first (especially general sections such as GENERAL TIPS, LUBRICATION, and BEARINGS), then use specific sections as you need them. If I call things by names that are unfamiliar — refer to the diagrams.

Although bikes have been around a long time and the basics remain the same, there are always new improvements — and new fads — and certainly many variations on the old stand-bys and many brand names. So if the equipment on your bike doesn't fit exactly with the diagrams in this book, find the closest thing and go from there. For simplicity, I'll sometimes use the term 10 speed when the information actually applies to 5-24 speed derailleur bikes as well.

People approach repair problems differently. Some will replace a whole part or even a whole bike if there is a problem. Others, because of their temperament or necessity will try to fix whatever is broken or replace as few parts as possible. I've always leaned towards replacing as little as possible and trying to fix most anything. While I can't cover every possible problem on every possible brand name and model of every part, I do try to give some extra detail for those who don't want or can't afford to just throw away problem parts.

HOW TO CARE FOR YOUR BIKE. Keep your bike clean, lubricated, and adjusted. Bikes have a lot of moving parts. Grit, lack of lubrication, and poor adjustment can ruin parts fast. On the other hand, if kept in good shape they should last long. Be aware of your bike and any unusual sounds or feelings. You can often catch (and fix) problems before they become serious. Don't let any part continually scrunch or rub. It will get worn out.

GOOD LUCK fixing your bike.

And ride safely.

TOOLS

The main tools you will need to fix your bike are wrenches and a screwdriver. Wrenches should preferably be a set of wrenches, open end or combination. Most bikes use metric wrenches. If your bike uses metric wrenches, don't try to get by with the inch wrenches you had for your old Chevy. Although a few sizes will correspond, others won't.

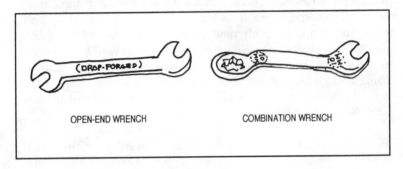

OPEN-END WRENCH   COMBINATION WRENCH

An adjustable crescent wrench (6" is a good size) will work but it can easily strip nuts (round the corners) if you aren't careful. Socket wrenches work well in some spots and some places use allen (hexagonal or hex) wrenches.

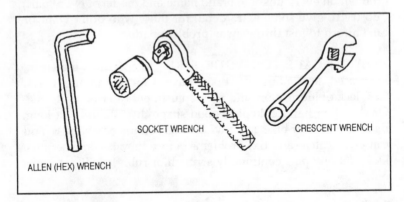

SOCKET WRENCH   CRESCENT WRENCH

ALLEN (HEX) WRENCH

You'll also need screwdrivers — big and little if you have them. Check your bike; you may also need a Phillips screwdriver (the head looks like (+)).

A spoke wrench to adjust spokes (they come in different sizes, get one that fits your spoke nipples), a cone spanner (thin wrench) to adjust hubs, tire levers to remove tires, and an air pressure gauge are all inexpensive and worth having.

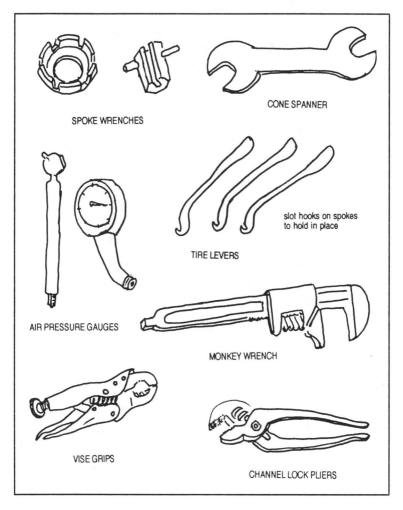

SPOKE WRENCHES

CONE SPANNER

AIR PRESSURE GAUGES

TIRE LEVERS

slot hooks on spokes to hold in place

MONKEY WRENCH

VISE GRIPS

CHANNEL LOCK PLIERS

Vise grips are handy for various things, but use them very carefully — they are powerful and can easily scrunch things. Channel lock pliers and a monkey wrench can also come in handy.

If you have a freewheel (5-24 speed bikes), you'll need a freewheel remover to take it off (make sure to get one that fits your particular freewheel). If you have cotterless cranks, you'll need a crank puller. If you have to change the length of your chain, or simply to take it off on most 10-speeds, you may need a chain tool. You may also want wire cutters (to cut cables), a thin pedal wrench (for pedals), chain whips (to remove freewheel sprockets), a lockring wrench and a pin wrench for bottom bracket. There are more special tools available, but often you can improvise.

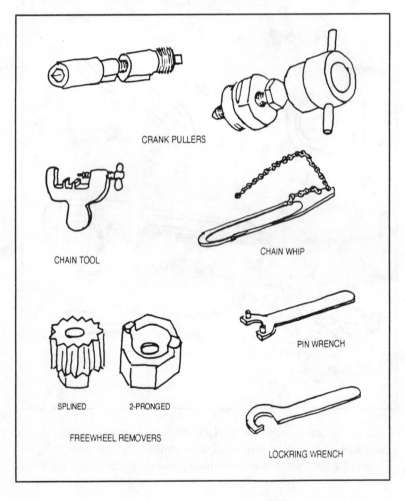

CRANK PULLERS

CHAIN TOOL

CHAIN WHIP

SPLINED   2-PRONGED

FREEWHEEL REMOVERS

PIN WRENCH

LOCKRING WRENCH

Your tool kit for home or trips should also include some parts such as brake rubbers, brake and gear cables, a spare tube — and a tire patch kit. And this book.

On tools: expensive ones are usually stronger and more durable than cheap ones. If you can and if you'll use them a lot, buy a good set of wrenches and cone spanner.

GENERAL TIPS

Here are some general things you should know.

BE GENTLE. Big huge nuts can be tightened with lots of strength but little ones can't — the threads will strip or the bolt will break.

USE THE RIGHT SIZE WRENCH. The wrong size wrench (or a crescent wrench that's too loose) can round the edges of a bolt or nut, making it hard for a wrench to get a grip next time. Wrong size screwdrivers can mess up screw heads too.

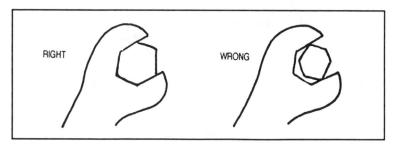

TURN WRENCHES THE CORRECT WAY (to lessen chances of stripping nuts or breaking wrenches). Turn so the pressure is on the most solid arm.

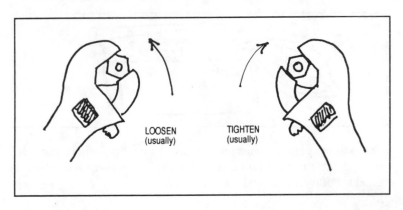

LOOSEN
(usually)

TIGHTEN
(usually)

RIGHT AND LEFT HAND THREAD. Bolts (and screws and nuts) almost always <u>tighten clockwise </u>and <u>loosen counter-clockwise</u>. This is "**right-hand thread**." Parts in some places have "left-hand thread" and tighten counter-clockwise. The left pedal and sometimes the right hanger cup and lockring have left-hand thread. This is so the natural pedaling motion doesn't unscrew them.

CHANGING PARTS. Parts on bicycles are generally interchangeable and all you need to know is how different parts are attached. But sometimes parts are not inter-changeable or not easily interchangeable so you need to know what fits together and what doesn't. Sometimes changing one thing will mean you'll have to change another. For example, changing the size of your chainwheel or rear sprockets may mean changing the length of your chain as well. So before you begin to change things around, make sure the new parts will fit. If you're buying new parts to fit on old ones, take the old ones to the store with you, or take the whole bike.

SIZE STANDARDS DIFFER — for different kinds of bikes and different countries — so beware if you are changing parts. Watch for different diameters and/or threads of handlebars, handlebar stems, forks, hangers, headsets, pedals, and spokes.

12

THREADS DIFFER. Different countries use different threads (different thicknesses and number of threads per inch) on bolts and such. When you replace a nut, make sure it has the same thread as the bolt. If it doesn't go on easily — don't force it. That's a good sign that the threads are different and you'll strip them. The main kinds of threads are American, French, Italian, and English (also used on Japanese parts).

LOCKNUTS (or lockrings) tighten down on nuts or cones to make the nut or cone stay in place. Usually the nut or cone adjusts something and its exact position is important. To tighten a locknut: hold the nut with one wrench in the position you want it, then tighten the locknut down on it with another wrench. You may have a lockwasher to help keep the cone in place. They usually have a "key" ⊚ that fits in a grove and lets them slide up and down but not turn.

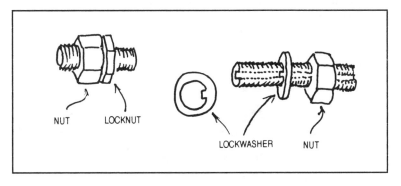

NUT   LOCKNUT   LOCKWASHER   NUT

LIQUID WRENCH or other "penetrating oil" loosens tight joints. Nut stuck on tight? Squirt some on, give it time to soak in, tap gently to help it get inside, then try.

GREASE THREADS routinely before putting nuts on. This will make it easier to remove the nut at some future time.

METAL FATIGUE. Something happens to metal when it's bent or pounded on too much or the wrong way (the molecules get messed up or something) and it's weakened. So if you must do those things to your bike, be aware you may have weaker metal under you.

CLEANING

Periodically you should take your bike apart, clean it thoroughly, and re-pack the bearings with grease. I grew up and then went to college in the northeast and every year the first warm sunny spring day was my "spring cleaning" day. I'd spread my tools out, usually on the sidewalk, and start taking things apart. By the end of the day, my bike was ready for another year of heavy use.

CLEANING. Get all the grit and dirty grease out. A solvent like kerosene cuts grease. Sometimes you want to just dump parts in a can of kerosene and let them soak. Sometimes it's nice to have a small squirt can full of kerosene so you can squirt and wash away dirt in hard to reach places. A toothbrush or small, stiff paintbrush can help scrape dirt off. Wipe clean and let dry. Drying is important because if you add new grease before the kerosene has completely evaporated, the kerosene will wash away the new grease. Chains can be taken off and soaked in kerosene.

DO NOT get oil (or grease, kerosene, Liquid Wrench, etc.) on rubber. They all eat rubber.

You might want to take the whole bike apart at once (careful to keep each set of parts separate), clean it all, and then re-assemble. Or you might want to clean one part and put it back together again before going on to the next (being very careful not to get kerosene on any newly greased areas!) Tape parts together with masking tape or draw pictures if you're afraid you'll forget the order of things. An egg carton can keep screws and parts neatly sorted.

LUBRICATION

Bikes have moving parts — where metal rubs against metal. Most of those places (headset, bottom bracket, hubs, pedals, gears) have bearings to reduce friction. You want those joints to be smooth.

Use grease to lubricate the big places with bearings (headset, bottom bracket, hubs, pedals, and gears). Put grease inside gear and brake cable casings to let the cables slide more easily. Graphite, teflon, or silicone based lubricants work well on chains, hand brakes, derailleurs, and other exposed places. Lubricate often, maybe once a month or after you've been in the rain. Oil, which will attract dirt, should not be used on exposed places and should be reserved for the insides of 3-speed hubs and freewheels. Bearings packed with grease should be taken apart, cleaned, and re-packed with grease at least once a year. Places with grease fittings can be greased with a small grease gun.

Grit and dirt crunch around, wear out parts, and make them sticky and uneven. The bike is built to make it hard for dirt to get inside but it will, especially if nearby areas are dirty or if parts are loose. Oil also tends to attract dirt. So keep your bike clean and adjusted. If your seat post is open on top, cover it with tape to keep dirt out (and to keep the dirt from going down inside the frame to the bottom bracket!)

DON'T get kerosene or oil on rubber, i.e. tires or brake rubbers (remember, it eats rubber).

LUBRICATION CHECK LIST:

Grease (once a year) — headset, hanger, pedals, hubs, and cables.
Lubricate (once a month) — derailleurs, chain, and hand brakes.
Oil — 1 & 3-speed hub (with oil fitting) and freewheel.

BEARINGS

Several parts of the bike have bearings — headset, hubs, bottom bracket, pedals, rear derailleur wheels.

BALL BEARINGS are a series of steel balls. Instead of metal scrunching or sliding directly against another metal surface, the balls roll in between to reduce friction.

Bearings are usually found in matched pairs — except on pedals where there are sometimes different amounts of balls at either end because the pedal axle is tapered.

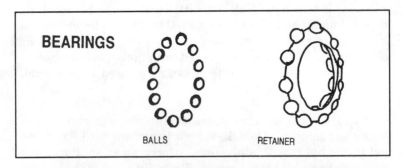

BEARINGS

BALLS   RETAINER

RETAINERS. Sometimes the balls are loose, sometimes they are held in a circle by a metal or plastic ring, called a retainer or cage, leaving the balls free to turn. Retainers are much easier to work with — you don't have to worry about a whole mess of balls rolling all over the floor when you take something apart. But be careful, some balls may fall out. The retainer part sometimes breaks — sometimes just enough to let a ball or two fall out, sometimes it gets totally chewed up and all you have is balls and a few metal fragments. If it's broken, get another one. You can also replace a retainer with just balls — use the same size balls as were in the retainer, just add more. Notice the way the retainer goes in. Only the balls (and not the retainer cage) should touch the **races** (the cups or cones that go on either side of the balls). When you replace a retainer, make sure to get the grease well inside the cage, around the balls.

16

HOW MANY BALLS? If you have loose balls, it's sometimes hard to know how many you should have. The rule of thumb is: one less than it takes to fill the space. Consider how the balls will be when the parts are together. Will the balls be pushed to the outside of the cup? If so, count how many balls it takes to fill the space with the balls pushed to the outside. Grease will hold the balls in position.

Write it down. When you take something apart with balls, do it very carefully. Count the balls in each place and write it down. If you find different size balls in corresponding places (such as both sides of a hub), something is wrong (except, as I said, for some pedals). Change it. Make sure you have the right amount of balls — they are cheap but important.

A hint on replacing balls. Grease the place where they are to go first — then you can just set the balls in place (on the greased end of a screwdriver for hard-to-reach places) and they stay where they should.

WORN BEARINGS. Bearings are worn (and need to be replaced) if the balls are rusty, pitted, or not smooth; the retainer (if there is one) is broken or bent; or the races (the cups or cones that go on either side of the balls) are pitted or not smooth (in which case you have to replace the races too). Bearings are cheap. If in any doubt, replace them. If you need to replace any of the balls in one set, or add some to fill the space properly, replace all the balls in that set. The balls need to be exactly the same.

ADJUSTING BEARINGS. The basic principle is to tighten the adjusting cone or cup (whatever part holds the bearings in place) until the part turns freely but without extra play. Try different adjustments — after a while you'll get the feel of it. Wheel bearings in the hub are easy ones to learn on — it's pretty easy to feel scrunching and extra play when you hold the axle in both hands and spin the wheel. Try tightening the cone until it's snug (never use force, you'll damage the bearings or races!) and then backing off slowly, testing often. The place where it stops scrunching when it spins should be the right place (probably about 1/8 turn back). Tightening a locknut or lockring down can change the bearing adjustment, so hold the cone while you tighten the locknut and check when you're done to make sure the adjustment is still right.

SEALED BEARINGS. There are two types of sealed bearings: sealed mechanism and cartridge bearings. These are designed to need less lubrication and adjustment than regular bearings. Sealed bearings are not magic — don't soak them in water.

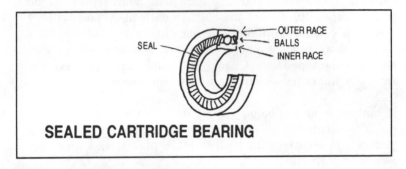

SEAL — OUTER RACE / BALLS / INNER RACE

SEALED CARTRIDGE BEARING

Sealed cartridge bearings have balls and races together in one unit with a built-in seal to hold in the grease. They are not adjustable and are meant to last a long time. On some the seal can be removed (gently) so you can add more grease but most are totally sealed and should just be replaced when they fail.

Sealed mechanism (adjustable) bearings are just like a normal bearing but are sealed with an "O" ring and/or a thick dustcap. They are overhauled like regular bearings. Add grease under the seal when you re-assemble.

SLEEVE BEARINGS. Some places (some derailleur wheels and pedals) have "sleeve" bearings instead of ball bearings. That's just a smooth metal or plastic band. Clean and lubricate like ball bearings.

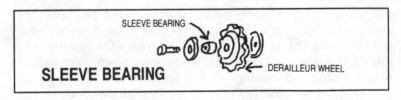

SLEEVE BEARING

SLEEVE BEARING

DERAILLEUR WHEEL

ADJUSTMENTS
& OVERHAUL

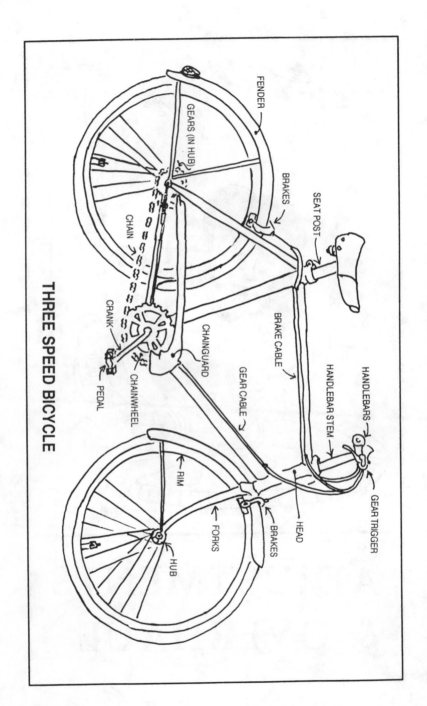

THREE SPEED BICYCLE

FENDER

GEARS (IN HUB)

BRAKES

SEAT POST

CHAIN

CRANK

PEDAL

CHAINWHEEL

CHAINGUARD

BRAKE CABLE

GEAR CABLE

HANDLEBAR STEM

HANDLEBARS

GEAR TRIGGER

RIM

FORKS

BRAKES

HEAD

HUB

TIRES

AIR. Keep tires pumped up. Tires usually say on them how much air they hold but here's an idea:

27 x 1 1/8 — 85-100 lbs.	26 x 1.75 — 40-65 lbs.
27 x 1 1/4 — 60-85 lbs.	20 x 1.75 — 30-50 lbs.
26 x 1 3/8 — 40-60 lbs.	26 x 2.125 — 30-65 lbs.
700 x 20C — 85-110 lbs.	

Cheap or old tires will usually not hold as much air pressure as new or expensive ones. Heavier people should have more air in their tires than little skinny people.

Too much air can cause the tube to burst out from under the tire and a blowout (which means a new tube and maybe a new tire if the blowout stretched the wire around the edge of the tire). Very full tires will give you a hard, bumpy ride. Too little air causes more friction between the bike and the road which will cause the tire to wear faster and maybe crack on the sides. The wheel rim will also be less protected and more liable to be bent by bumps in the road. Beware of gas station air pumps — they fill tires very fast and gauges often don't work right so it's very easy to blow out a tire. Air pressure goes down with time so check your tires regularly. If you have to refill your tires often, the tube may just be old and you need a new one.

VALVE LEAKS. Check the tire valve for leaks. Holding the valve facing up, put a few drops of water (soapy water is even better — or spit if you're on the road) inside. If you see bubbles form, you have a leak.

If the valve leaks, you can tighten it by screwing the inside part (valve core) in more. Valve caps often have a little thing on the end for this, as do some pressure gauges. If yours doesn't, borrow or buy one. You can also buy new valve cores if yours breaks, but better yet, take one out from the next tube you throw away (just unscrew it with your valve cap) and keep it for a spare.

PRESTA VALVES are found mainly on lightweight high-performance bikes. They need special pumps or a "valve adapter" to let regular pumps fit. To put air in, loosen the core locknut (A), tap it downward if necessary, then use the pump. Screw the locknut back down when you're done.

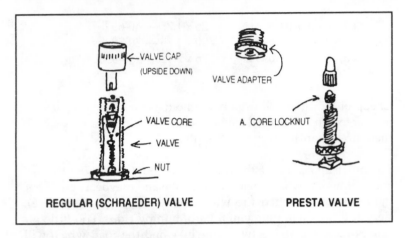

FLATS. To patch a flat tire you don't have to remove the wheel (though that is usually easier, see p. 26) or even the tire.

TO REMOVE TUBE. Pry out one side of the tire all around and pull out the tube. Careful. Don't use a screwdriver to pry; you're likely to just get one more hole. There are special "tire levers" made of metal or plastic but blunt plier handles or spoon handles will do (use plastic levers for aluminum hubs). Tire levers usually have a little hook on the other end so you can hook it around a spoke and free up a hand once it's in place. Put one tire lever in and pry out the tire (careful not to pinch the tube). Put the second lever in 3-4" away and pry out the tire at that point. Repeat with the third lever if necessary. By then you should be able to push one lever the rest of the way around. Be very careful not to poke or pinch the tube. Go easy on the tire too. There's a metal wire (the "bead") around the edge which can stretch or break and then the tire won't stay on well (and you'll need to replace it). It may help to loosen the bead of the tire all around, then push it in to the deepest part of the rim which will give you a little more slack at one end.

22

To find the hole, blow up the tire and listen and feel for the leak. If that fails to locate the leak, hold the tube under water and watch for bubbles.

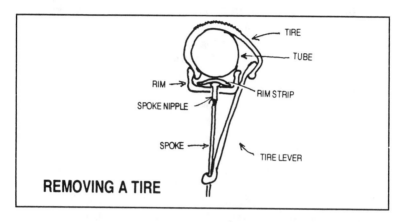

REMOVING A TIRE

TIRE PATCH KITS usually come with instructions. For regular patches: clean the area well, roughen the surface with some kind of buffer (sandpaper will do), put on the glue and let it dry slightly, put on the patch and press it down well, working away from the center of the patch. Dust a little talcum (baby) powder on the tube to keep extra glue from glueing the tube to the tire.

Before you put the newly patched tube back in the tire, check to make sure there is no glass or nail left in the tire. Put the tube back in place, putting the valve through the valve hole first and then working in both directions away from the valve hole. If you're putting in a brand new tube, put a little air in it first to unfold it and give it some shape.

When the tube is in place (and not twisted) you can put the tire back on. Be careful — the tire levers can easily pinch the tube and make a hole. If you can push the tire back on without levers, do so. Push the tire with your thumbs or palms, starting near the valve and working away from it in both directions. When the tire is on the rim, push the valve up into the tire, seat the tire well seated around it, and then pull the valve out again. Now pump up the tire, carefully.

Tires sometimes tend to come out of the rim when the tubes are blown up to the proper pressure (and, of course, when blown up too much). This can be due to the extra thickness of the tube near the valve, old and tired or cheap tires, a stretched wire on the tire edge due to a blowout or rough handling while changing a flat, or dented rims. When it happens, try letting out some of the air, pushing the tire back in where it came out and holding it there while you pump up the tire slowly. Does it still come out? You may need a new tire or straighter rims but this method often works, at least as a stop-gap measure.

If it happens around the valve, push the valve up into the tire a little and make sure the tire fits well around the tube at that point. Then pull the valve out again and pump up the tire.

WORN TIRES. Wear on the side of the tire is probably due to the frame or brake rubber rubbing against the tire. If it's the frame, loosen the axle nuts and center the wheel. If it's the brake rubbers, they should hit on the rim, not the tire (see p. 52). Cracks on the side of the tire are probably due to under-inflation.

BALD SPOTS on the tire tread can be caused by the brakes catching on a blip in the rim and always stopping the tire in the same spot (see BLIPS, p. 29).

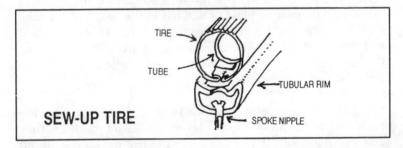

TIRE

TUBE

TUBULAR RIM

SPOKE NIPPLE

SEW-UP TIRE

SEW-UP (TUBULAR) TIRES are fancy, lightweight tires with the tire sewn up around the tube and glued to the rim. They are also much harder to patch. You have to unglue the tire from the rim, find the leak, unsew the tire at that point, patch, sew, and glue.

TIRE SAVERS (used mainly on 10-speeds with sew-up or thin tread tires — they don't work on big knobby tires) are pieces of wire that attach where the brake bolts on (brakes with a center bolt). They knock off pieces of glass and such before they dig in and cause a flat. They work!

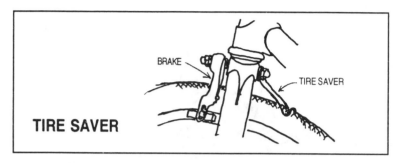

TIRE SAVER

RIM STRIPS are rubber or cloth strips that go around the rim between the rim and the tube (see p. 23). They protect the tube from spokes that might stick through the rim. Make sure you have them.

WHEELS

Wheels should be firmly attached to the frame and centered (otherwise they'll wobble or rub). If you can wiggle the wheel sideways with your hand, see if the axle nuts that hold the wheel to the frame are tight. If they are and the wheel still wiggles, you'll probably need to **adjust the cones in the hub** (see p. 32). If the wheel wobbles only when it's turning, you probably need to **"true" the wheel** (adjust the tightness of the spokes to take out the wobble and make the wheel round) (p. 38) or **straighten blips** in the rim (p.29). If you have missing spokes, you'll also need to **replace the spokes** before trying to true the wheel (see p. 32). If your rim is too warped or bent or has bad kinks, you may not be able to straighten it and you will have to take the rim off and **replace the rim** (see p. 33). You'll often need to **remove the wheel** to do other things. That's usually easier to do with the bike upside down.

TO REMOVE A WHEEL. For the front wheel, simply loosen the axle nuts. You may need to use wrenches on both sides at once. Hold one side steady while you turn the other.

If you have **quick release levers** instead of nuts, flip the lever to release the wheel.

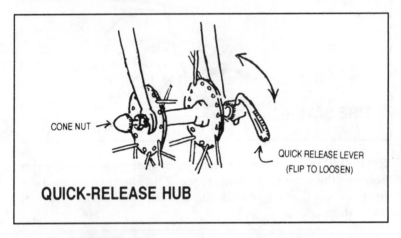

CONE NUT →

QUICK RELEASE LEVER
(FLIP TO LOOSEN)

QUICK-RELEASE HUB

If you have hand brakes and they seem to hold the wheel in once you've loosened the axle nuts or quick-release lever, just pull and wiggle the wheel past them if you can. For fat tires you'll need to do more. If you have a quick-release unit on the brakes (see p. 50) loosen that to pull the wheel out more easily. You may also be able to hold the brakes in with your hand and unhook the brake stirrup cable (if you have one, see p. 50) to loosen the brake. You can also let some air out of the tire or remove a brake shoe to make the wheel easier to pull out. If all else fails, loosen the cable anchor bolt (but don't let the cable slip all the way out).

Rear wheels usually have an extra thing to do.

For **rear derailleurs**, after you've loosened the axle nuts, just pull the derailleur towards the rear of the bike (preferably with the chain on the small sprocket) and pull the wheel out. Notice how the chain goes around the derailleur wheels so you can get it back in right.

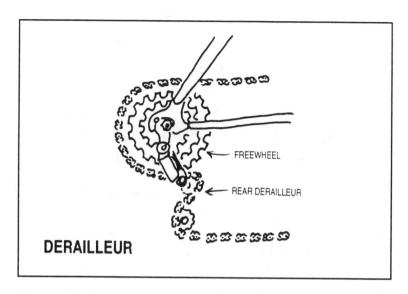

FREEWHEEL

REAR DERAILLEUR

DERAILLEUR

For **coaster brake** wheels, undo the nut (A) that attaches the brake arm to the frame.

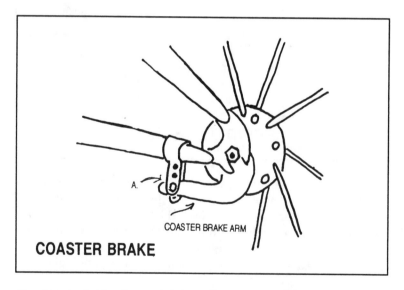

A.

COASTER BRAKE ARM

COASTER BRAKE

For **3-speed** wheels, undo the adjusting barrel (B) on the gear cable. Leave the locknut (C) in place so you'll know how far to screw the adjusting barrel when you replace the wheel.

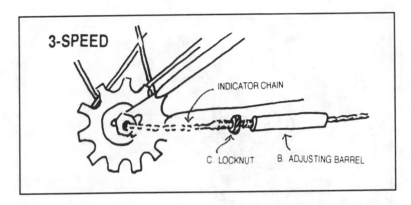

3-SPEED

INDICATOR CHAIN

C. LOCKNUT   B. ADJUSTING BARREL

TO REPLACE THE WHEEL. Do the opposite of what you just did. Washers, if you have them, usually go on the outside of the frame, right before the axle nuts. Hold the wheel centered in the frame as you tighten the axle nuts.

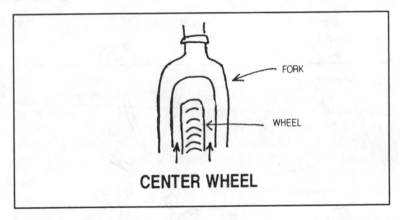

FORK

WHEEL

CENTER WHEEL

For **quick release levers,** just flip the lever. If that doesn't tighten the wheel enough, loosen the lever, screw in the wing nut or cone nut on the other side or the hub (see p. 26) until it's snug (with the lever loose) then flip the lever in again. You want the lever tight enough so it's pretty hard to lock in position. If it's too loose, it won't hold your wheel on tight.

For **coaster brake and 3-speed rear wheels,** pull the wheel back so there is about 1/2" - 3/4" play in the chain (keeping the wheel centered at the same time) Get the nuts tight.

28

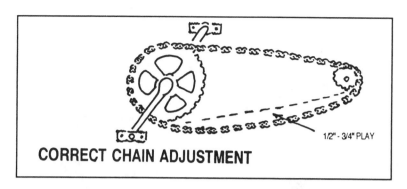

CORRECT CHAIN ADJUSTMENT

1/2" - 3/4" PLAY

For **3-speed rear wheels**, re-attach the adjusting barrel, screwing the barrel to where you left the nut. Tighten the locknut down tight. Check to see if the gears are adjusted correctly (see p. 71).

For **coaster brakes**, make sure the brake arm faces the right way so you can hook it up. Attach the brake arm securely to the frame with nut (A) (see p. 27).

WHEEL BLIPS. If there are blips (bulges in the rim) you want to take out, you may be able to straighten them (carefully!) with vise grips, channel lock pliers, or a C-clamp. Blips are bad if they are big enough to make it impossible to true the wheel, if the tire refuses to stay in the rim at that point (and pops out and you get a blowout), or if the brake pads catch on the blip and always stop the rim at the same place (which will lead to a worn spot on the tire and finally a hole).

TO STRAIGHTEN BLIP. Adjust the vice grips so they are snug on a normal section of the rim. Then put them over the blip. Slowly squeeze the vice grips. If adjusted correctly to begin with, the vice grips should lock at the point where the blip is flattened out. If the blip remains, tighten the vice grips slightly and try again. Go slowly — you don't want to replace the blip with an indentation. It's best to do this after you take off the tire and tube but you can do it with the tire on. If the tire is off, you can place a small block of wood inside the rim to prevent tightening too much. If the blip is only on one side, protect the other side with a piece of wood.

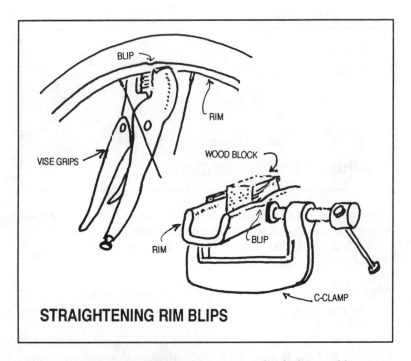

STRAIGHTENING RIM BLIPS

Blips and dents come from riding over curbs, holes, and bumps. Avoid that, especially with narrow wheels and tires. Mountain bike wheels are usually reinforced to minimize this kind of damage. If you get dents regularly (maybe you are tall or heavy or ride bumpy roads) it might be worth putting more solid rims on your bike. Maybe you just need more air in your tires.

HUB

TO TAKE WHEEL HUB APART. Front hubs are simple. Take the wheel off the bike and remove the outer axle nut (A) and washer (B) on one side. If there is no washer (preferably a serrated grip washer), get one soon — your wheel will stay in place better. You only have to undo one side of the hub unless you are replacing a stripped or bent axle.

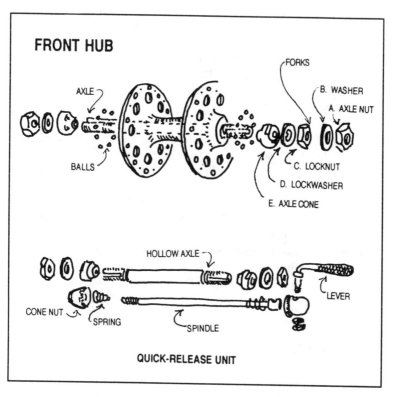

FRONT HUB

FORKS

AXLE

B. WASHER

A. AXLE NUT

BALLS

C. LOCKNUT

D. LOCKWASHER

E. AXLE CONE

HOLLOW AXLE

LEVER

CONE NUT

SPRING

SPINDLE

QUICK-RELEASE UNIT

Hold the axle cone (E) with a cone spanner (a very thin wrench) and loosen locknut (C). Remove the locknut, lockwasher (D) and axle cone (E). Once the cone is out, the bearings will come out, either loose balls or retainers. As with other bearings, holding the hub over a box or rag will help keep the balls from rolling all over and getting lost. Count the balls. Pull out the axle from the other end to get the rest of the ball bearings — and count them. Clean the bearings and hub, check for a bent axle, damaged threads on the axle, or worn or missing parts. Grease, re-assemble, and adjust.

For **"quick release"** hubs, unscrew the cone-shaped nut on the side opposite the lever and pull out the quick-release assembly that goes through the axle and then proceed. When putting it back, make sure the little springs face the right way (small part inward).

REAR HUBS will have extra stuff, either a coaster brake or 3-speed gears inside the hub or a sprocket or freewheel next to it, but they also have bearings like the front hub and you can get to them without messing with the other stuff. Be very careful with the kerosene as you clean the hub so you don't get it on the other parts.

TO ADJUST HUBS. Turn the adjusting cone (E) until there is no extra play but the wheel still turns freely. Hold the wheel in front of you with one hand on each end of the axle and spin the wheel. If it scrunches, it's too tight. Hold the wheel and wiggle the axle. If it wiggles, it's too loose. When it's just right, put lockwasher (D) in position and tighten locknut (C) (while holding the cone with the cone spanner so it doesn't change position). Spin the wheel again to make sure it's right. Remember that tightening down the locknut may change the adjustment so check it carefully.

SPOKES

Spokes can be easy to put in. The hardest part is getting enough room to get the spoke through its little hole and to its proper place on the rim without bending it all up. To get some 10-speed spokes in you have to remove the freewheel, which is usually on very tight and requires a special tool (see p. 84). Sprockets on 1 and 3-speed bikes are easier to get off. Most are held on by a round wire clip. Pry it off with a screwdriver (see p. 73).

REPLACING A SPOKE. If you're just replacing a spoke, you still have to take off the tire, tube, and rim strip to put the spoke nipple in. If the nipple is still in place you don't, although it's probably a good idea to let the air out of the tire. Take out the old broken spoke and get the correct size replacement. Spokes come in a lot of different sizes; measure another spoke carefully. All spokes on a wheel should be the same size.

Put the spoke through the empty hole in the hub, with the head facing the opposite way from the spokes on either side of it. Make the spoke go to the proper hole on the rim, weaving it over and under other spokes if your wheel works that way. Put the spoke nipple on and screw it down. The nipple works like a nut and you can use a screwdriver (from above, if the nipple has a slot in it), spoke wrench, or if it's absolutely necessary an adjustable crescent wrench (though this should be just for emergencies as it can strip the nipple).

Make sure the wheel is true (see p. 38) and no spokes stick up through the nipples. Cut off and file down any extra spoke that sticks through. Replace the rim strip, tube, and tire. Make sure you have a rim strip.

SPOKING A WHEEL

Here's the procedure for taking off a rim and putting on a new one or building up a wheel from scratch (when you have a hub, spokes, and rim). This is not meant to be a complete guide to wheel-building but it will get the job done.

Before you take anything apart — take a good look at how the wheel is "laced" — how the spokes go, the pattern they make. How many spokes does each one cross? Do they go over and under? Is it the same as your other wheel? If so, you can use that as a model.

TAKING OFF THE RIM. Take off the tire, tube, and rim strip. If you have a freewheel, remove it at this point (see p. 84). It is much harder to remove the freewheel after the spokes are removed. Next you want to undo all the spokes. The nipple that goes through the rim screws on to the spoke. Unscrew them all — but read on to the end of this section first! Lubricating the nipples will make the job easier. For tight, rusted ones, squirt in Liquid Wrench. Careful, you can break a good spoke trying to unscrew the nipple. Also make sure you unscrew in the right direction — counter-clockwise as you look at the <u>head</u> of the nipple (careful though, you often look at it from the other end). If your spokes are rusty or bent and need replacing, you can just clip them all with a wire cutter.

If you are just replacing the rim, you'll save a lot of time and trouble by not messing up the order of the spokes. Loosen all the nipples until they are almost off. Then put the wheel down flat and lay the new rim on top of the old one, lining up the valve hole and making sure the offset holes (if you have them) correspond. Tie the two rims together in 2-3 places. Doing one spoke at a time, take the nipple the rest of the way off and move the spoke to the hole in the new rim right above the hole in the old rim. Start the nipple on. Do all the rest of the spokes the same way. Skip to TIGHTEN NIPPLES, p. 38.

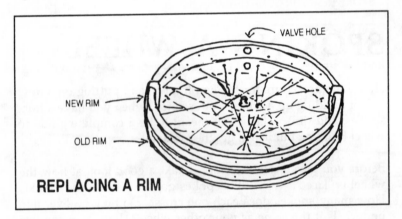

REPLACING A RIM

On some rims the holes are "offset" — not all in a straight line. Spokes from one side of the hub should go to rim holes on the same side.

BUILDING A WHEEL. If you are building a wheel from scratch you have to decide what size spokes to use and how to lace it. A good way to decide is to find a similar wheel with the same size rim and hub (there are small flange and large flange hubs). Measure those spokes and lace your wheel the same way. One way to lace a wheel is to have each spoke go under 3 others and over 1 (or over 3 and under 1, depending on how you look at it) so it crosses four spokes in all.

There are different ways to get the spokes in and to their proper place on the rim — here's the one I like best.

PUT SPOKES IN through the hub alternating one spoke going in and one going out. If your hub has holes that are countersunk on one side, the spoke heads go on the <u>non-countersunk</u> side (the countersunk part is for the bend in the spoke, not the head of the spoke).

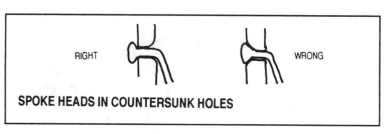

RIGHT   WRONG

SPOKE HEADS IN COUNTERSUNK HOLES

Lay the hub and spokes on the floor with one end of the hub up and the spokes fanned out around. It'll be a mess — patience.

LACING THE WHEEL. The spokes belong in four groups (see diagram on p. 36):

   (A) spokes going down from the top part of the hub (heads out)
   (B) spokes going up from the top part of the hub (heads in)
   (C) spokes going up from the bottom part of the hub (heads out)
   (D) spokes going down from the bottom part of the hub (heads in)

Put one spoke from group (A) in the rim and start the nipple. Start it preferably in the first hole counter-clockwise from the valve hole (this will leave space for the air pump) but any hole will do (any hole towards the top if you have offset holes in the rim).

Put the rest of the (A) spokes in the rim, going to every 4th hole (skip 3 in between). Turn the rim so the spokes are going clockwise if that hasn't already happened naturally.

35

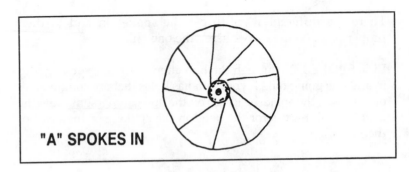

"A" SPOKES IN

Then put in all the (B) spokes, following the lacing pattern and going counter-clockwise. Remember your lacing pattern. Over 3, under 1? Then take a (B) spoke and move it counter-clockwise over three (A) spokes and then slip it under the 4th spoke you pass and into the middle hole on the rim between the 4th and 5th (A) spokes. Start the nipple on. When you're done, every other hole in the rim should be filled.

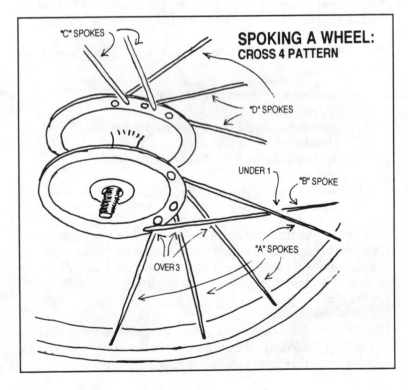

"C" SPOKES

SPOKING A WHEEL:
CROSS 4 PATTERN

"D" SPOKES

UNDER 1

"B" SPOKE

"A" SPOKES

OVER 3

Hold the loose spokes and turn the wheel over. Repeat what you just did for the (C) and then (D) spokes. The (C) spoke above (looking straight down at the wheel) a given (B) spoke should go next to that spoke on the rim. If it is a little counter-clockwise looking at the head of the spoke (it will not be exactly above), it should go in the next hole counter-clockwise to the (B) spoke on the rim.

Keep trying until the pattern is right and uniform. All the nipples should be started.

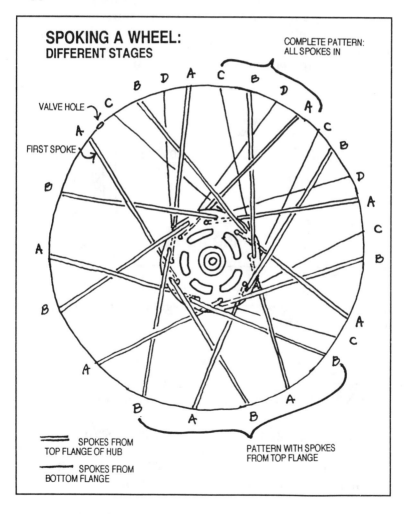

SPOKING A WHEEL:
DIFFERENT STAGES

COMPLETE PATTERN:
ALL SPOKES IN

VALVE HOLE

FIRST SPOKE

SPOKES FROM TOP FLANGE OF HUB

SPOKES FROM BOTTOM FLANGE

PATTERN WITH SPOKES FROM TOP FLANGE

TIGHTEN NIPPLES more, going around the rim in a circle. Try to do them evenly, like until the nipple reaches the end of the thread on the spokes. Then turn each one again, until all spokes seem tight. Don't tighten too much — that will pull the rim out of shape. If the spokes seem to be getting too tight, loosen the ones you've done a turn or two.

DISHING A WHEEL. For the rear wheel on a 10-speed, give the freewheel side spokes 3-4 extra turns as you are tightening the spokes. This "dishing the wheel" is to get the rim centered with respect to the frame even though the fat freewheel makes the hub not centered any more. If the spokes are already tight, loosen the non-freewheel ones 2 turns and tighten the freewheel side ones 2 turns (or until the rim is centered).

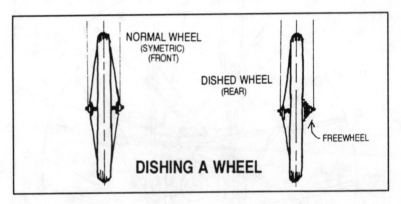

DISHING A WHEEL

The rim should be pretty straight now if you tightened the spokes evenly and began with a straight rim. In any case, now you true the wheel.

TRUEING A WHEEL

You can do this with the wheel on the bike. If the adjustment is minor, you can do it with the tire and tube on. If not, it's best to take them off. If the spoke gets tightened so much that it sticks through the nipple, it can puncture the tube. Rim strips are meant to protect the tube from this but they can't if a lot of spoke sticks through.

You can use your hand brakes to help true the wheel. Make sure the brake and wheel are centered in the frame (see pp. 53 and 28). Watch the brake rubbers as you spin the wheel slowly. If the wheel stays the same distance from the rubbers all the way around, your wheel is perfect. If not, wait until the rim gets to a place where it is closer to one side. Stop the wheel there. If you don't have hand brakes, watch where the rim passes through the frame. Put a chalk mark where the rim comes closer to one brake rubber. Or hold a piece of chalk near the rim first on one side and then the other and spin the wheel. Where the chalk hits the rim, the spokes need turning.

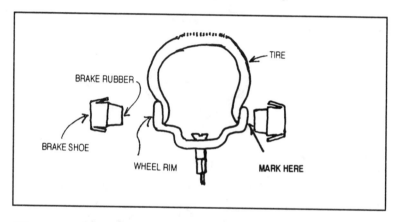

The principle of trueing a wheel is to loosen the spokes that go to the side of the hub that the rim pulls toward and tighten the spokes to the other side. Turn nipples to tighten or loosen spokes. Lubricate the nipples before you begin. Use Liquid Wrench if the nipples are tight (only if you've taken the tire, tube, and rim strip off, remember that it will eat tires). Let it soak in. If the spokes on the side the rim pulls towards are already loose, just tighten the other side. Otherwise loosen the nipple a turn and tighten the other side nipple a turn. Did that do anything? If not, try the same thing again. Do it little by little. Go one or two spokes in either direction from the one you just turned, turning the ones farther from the main spot less.

Nipples turn clockwise to tighten (normal way) as you look at the head of the nipple <u>but</u> when trueing a wheel you almost always look from the other direction. From that perspective clockwise loosens.

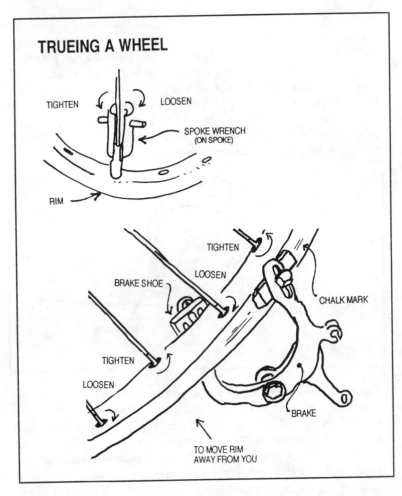

TRUEING A WHEEL

TIGHTEN   LOOSEN

SPOKE WRENCH
(ON SPOKE)

RIM

TIGHTEN

LOOSEN

BRAKE SHOE

CHALK MARK

TIGHTEN

LOOSEN

BRAKE

TO MOVE RIM
AWAY FROM YOU

Trueing a wheel can be frustrating work, especially if you are just learning. If you get tired, stop and come back later. If you get messed up, it may be easier to loosen all the spokes and start again (see TIGHTEN NIPPLES, p. 38). It gets easier with practice — even plain simple.

When you're done, check to make sure that the spokes don't stick out through the nipple inside the rim. If you just built the wheel (and started with a straight rim and the right size spokes) they shouldn't. If they do, see if you made a mistake. If not, clip or file off the extra. The tension on all the spokes should be fairly equal; check that. Then replace the rim strip, tube, and tire.

EGGS. The above should get out side-to-side wobble. Wheels also get out of round or even egg-shaped which is harder to deal with. For the point of an egg, tighten the spokes going to both sides of the hub from that part of the rim (turning spokes farther from the main spot less). For a flat spot, loosen the spokes to both sides of the hub.

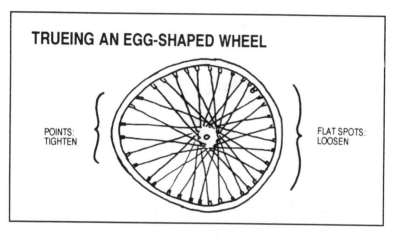

TRUEING AN EGG-SHAPED WHEEL

POINTS:
TIGHTEN

FLAT SPOTS:
LOOSEN

If you can't get out the wobble or egg by trueing, you need a new rim (see p. 33).

HANDLEBARS

Handlebars come in several different shapes but the adjustments are basically the same. The handlebars are held in place by a handlebar stem which fits in the frame.

TO ADJUST HANDLEBAR STEM. To change the height, you want to raise or lower the stem in the frame. Loosen the expander bolt (A) several turns (but not so much that the bolt comes out) then put a block of wood between the hammer and the expander bolt and bang it down into the handlebar stem. This should loosen the lug or wedge at the other end (B) and let you move the stem. Just loosening the expander bolt is useless — you have to bang it down. If you loosen the bolt too much, the wedge may just fall off inside the frame and you'll have to take off the stem and handlebars and turn the bike upside down to shake it out.

Once the handlebar stem is loose you can remove it or adjust the height. Once the height is set, just tighten the expander bolt.

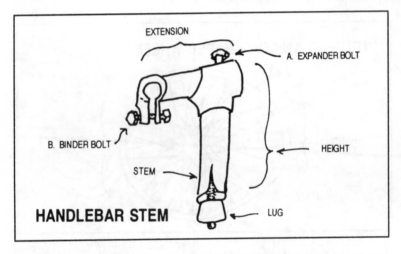

EXTENSION

A. EXPANDER BOLT

B. BINDER BOLT

HEIGHT

STEM

HANDLEBAR STEM

LUG

Always keep at least 2 1/2" of the stem in the frame. If your stem has a mark on it, don't raise it above the mark. If you need to raise the handlebars more, get a longer stem. Stems come in different sizes — different heights and different extensions so you can change the distance of the handlebars from you. (Seat placement also affects this, see p. 47.)

The expander bolt (A) also controls whether the handlebars are in line with the wheel. For loose handlebars (handlebars turn and the wheel doesn't or vise versa), tighten the expander bolt (A). If the wheel points one way and the handlebars another, loosen (A), straighten the handlebars, and re-tighten (A). If you can't tighten the handlebars enough, the expander bolt or wedge may be broken. Remove the handlebars and look at them.

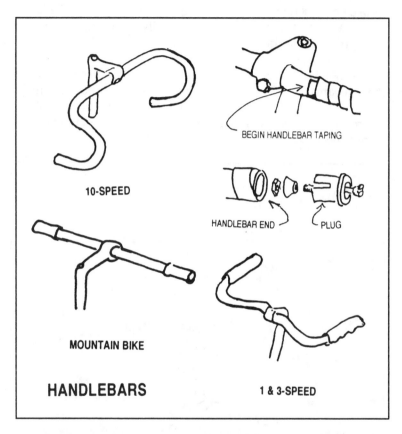

BEGIN HANDLEBAR TAPING

10-SPEED

HANDLEBAR END   PLUG

MOUNTAIN BIKE

HANDLEBARS   1 & 3-SPEED

HANDLEBARS IN STEM. The handlebars are held in the stem by a binder bolt (B) which also controls the tilt of the handlebars. If the handlebars are loose, tighten (B). If that doesn't tighten down enough, the binder bolt may be stripped or broken or the handlebars may be too small for the stem. You can get a shim (a thin piece of metal that fits around the center of the handlebars) if the handlebars are too small. For taped handlebars, see p. 56.

HEADSET

The head tube (where the front forks go through the frame) has bearings at either end, called the headset. These can be either loose balls or retainers. Take it apart carefully —the balls are small and tend to roll all over, especially since some come out upward and some downward.

TO TAKE HEADSET APART. Take out the handlebar stem and handlebars (see p. 42). As you do the next steps, hold the forks steady in the frame until the adjusting cone is all the way off — then you can deal with the balls. (If you have retainers, less care is needed.)

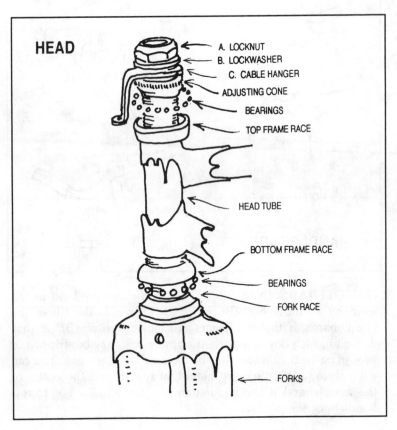

HEAD

A. LOCKNUT
B. LOCKWASHER
C. CABLE HANGER
ADJUSTING CONE
BEARINGS
TOP FRAME RACE

HEAD TUBE

BOTTOM FRAME RACE

BEARINGS
FORK RACE

FORKS

Loosen and remove locknut (A). Remove lockwasher (B) (which is likely to have a point that fits into a grove in the forks) and cable hanger (C) if you have one. Loosen and remove adjusting cone (D).

Still holding the fork in the frame, tilt the whole thing so the top set of balls (or retainer) falls into a neat pile. Hold the headset low over a rag or box to catch the balls. Count the balls. Then remove the forks and let the bottom set of balls fall into another neat pile and count them. There should be the same number top and bottom. If not, make sure there are when you put it back together again. If the balls all spilled immediately and got lost, don't panic. See p. 17 for how to figure out the number of balls.

Clean and check the bearings (balls or retainers) and races (the parts on either side of the bearings) for wear. Replace worn or missing parts — and adjust. Races can be pried or pushed off if necessary. They do not need to be removed unless worn or you're replacing the forks. All headset parts must match (diameter, type of thread, and curve of the races) so if you need to replace one part get an exact replacement or change the whole headset.

If you need to change the races on the head tube or forks, pry or push them off carefully with a screwdriver and put new ones on with a hammer and block of wood to protect the races.

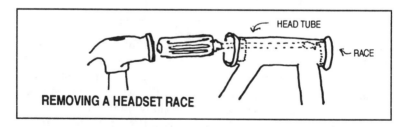

HEAD TUBE

RACE

REMOVING A HEADSET RACE

TO ADJUST THE HEADSET after you've taken it apart or if it's loose and the forks wobble inside the head tube. Tighten the adjusting cone down until the forks turn freely without extra play. Replace the lockwasher and locknut. If you have trouble getting rid of the looseness, take the headset apart and check to see if the bearings are in place.

SEAT

The main rule for seat and handlebar adjustment is to get them so that they are comfortable for you. Try different adjustments — those adjustments can make a big difference in how you feel on your bike. "Proper" or "suggested" adjustments are supposed to balance weight to lessen strain and increase efficiency. Since you can get used to different positions, it might be worth trying to get used to one that makes riding easier and is more beneficial for your body.

The suggested height for the seat is so that when you sit on it with the ball of your foot on the lower pedal, your knee is just slightly bent. Or so that your leg is straight with your heel on the pedal.

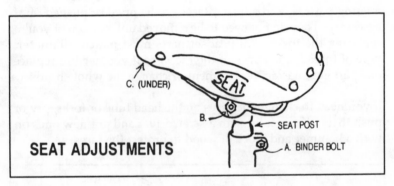

C. (UNDER)

B.

SEAT POST

SEAT ADJUSTMENTS

A. BINDER BOLT

TO ADJUST SEAT HEIGHT. The seat is attached to the seat post, which fits into the frame. You want to move the seat post. You don't need to remove the seat to do this. On most bikes the adjustment is made with a binder bolt (A) where the post goes into the frame. Some seat posts (especially mountain bikes) are held in by a quick release lever. Loosen the binder bolt nut or quick-release lever to remove or adjust the seat post. If it sticks, twist or bang the post.

If you remove the seat post, grease the part that goes inside the frame before re-inserting it. That will make it easier to move next time. You should always keep at least 2" of the post in the frame for stability. You can buy a longer seat post if you need to — just make sure you get the right diameter to fit your frame. If the diameter of the post is too small, use a shim.

If you can't get the quick-release lever tight enough after you replace the post, release the lever, tighten the cone nut on the other end a little(see p. 31), and re-tighten the lever.

MORE SEAT ADJUSTMENTS. There are two main kinds of seat posts: plain ones (with a separate several-part clamp to hold the seat) and seat posts with a built-in clamp on top for the seat. The clamps adjust both forward/back position and tilt. For plain posts with a separate clamp, there is a bolt (B) that holds the seat on the post. Loosen this to move the seat or tilt the seat up or down. Seat posts with a built-in clamp have bolts or allen screws (D) above or below the clamp to adjust seat position. Your seat should be pretty close to level. If you feel as though you are sliding off the seat or that you have too much pressure on your arms, tilt the nose up slightly.

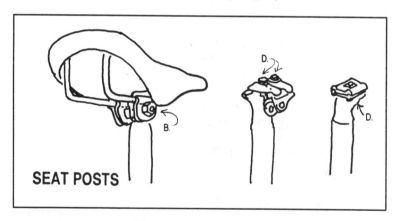

SEAT POSTS

Moving the seat forward or backward will change your position with relation to the pedals and the handlebars. Be picky — slight adjustments make a big difference.

Some leather seats have a nut under the front of the seat (C) that controls how taut or saggy the seat is. Saddle soap will soften up a stiff new leather seat.

47

FRAME

Frames come in different sizes — usually 17-25" for an adult bike. That's the distance from the bottom bracket axle to the top of the frame near the seat post. You should have a size that fits you, so you can stand comfortably straddling the top tube.

BENT FRAMES. Frames get bent, usually the forks and sometimes around the head tube or the rear stays.

The forks can be straightened. There is a fancy tool for this but a big piece of pipe slipped over the fork can do fine. Just put the pipe on the fork (the fork can be on the bike) to where it is bent and use your strength. The longer the pipe, the more leverage you'll have and the easier your job will be. Be gentle, you don't want to bend it too far. If you care about the paint, wrap rags around the forks first to protect them. Remember metal fatigue (see p. 13).

You can buy new forks. Some come in different lengths (know your frame size), some come long and need to be cut to size with a hacksaw. If you do this, screw the adjusting cone or locknut on the forks before you saw. When you take it off after, it will straighten out any threads damaged by the sawing. Threads on forks differ. Take along the headset locknut (that screws onto the forks) to match threads (or better yet, take the whole fork). To install new forks you'll need to take the headset apart (see p. 44).

Other bent parts can be straightened (even really bent ones). This is not recommended because of metal fatigue but it can be done. If you must do it, use brute force or try clamping the bike to something solid (like a 2 x 4).

The best solution for bent frames is prevention. Don't go smashing your bike into things, don't throw it down carelessly, and don't leave it lying down where it can get run over by a car. Treat your bike with care!

BRAKES

There are two main kinds of brakes:

COASTER BRAKE is a foot brake located on the rear hub and usually found on single speed bicycles but possible on 3-speeds. There is no simple adjustment for these. If they work poorly they need to be taken apart (see p. 57). Make sure the brake arm (the metal bar that comes out of the hub and bolts to the frame) is on tight. If there is an oil fitting or grease nipple on the hub, lubricate monthly.

HAND BRAKES, used on mountain bikes, 10-speeds and most 3-speeds, have hand levers on the handlebars that pull cables that pull rubber pads into contact with the wheel rim. There are five main types of hand brakes: center-pull (caliper), side-pull (caliper), cantilever, U-brakes, and cam brakes. All have several adjustments and many things that can go wrong.

COMMON HAND BRAKE PROBLEMS:

1) BRAKE SHOES may be too far from the rim so the brakes never catch well or too close so they rub when they shouldn't. The rubber brake pads (in the shoes) should be about 3/32" - 1/8" (3 mm) from the rim.

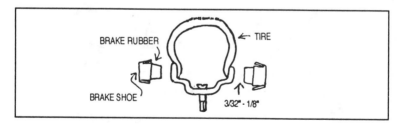

When there is a long "**adjusting barrel**" (A) (see p. 50-51) along the cable (either by the hand lever, by the brake, or on the cable hanger) use that for adjustment if possible. Screw it out (up) to tighten the cable and move the brake shoes closer to the rim. Move the locknut (F) to keep the barrel in the desired position.

49

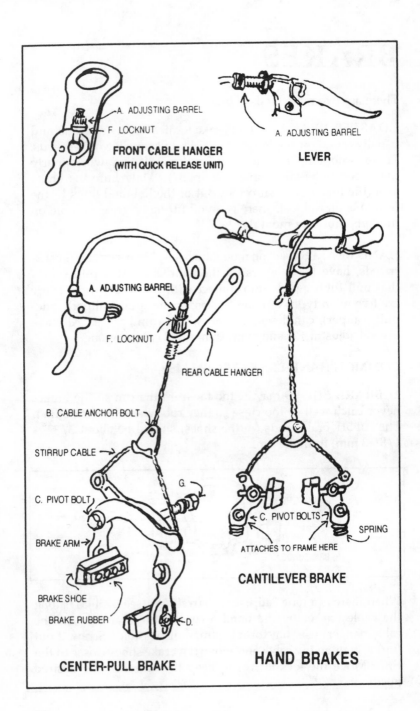

A. ADJUSTING BARREL
F. LOCKNUT
FRONT CABLE HANGER
(WITH QUICK RELEASE UNIT)

A. ADJUSTING BARREL
LEVER

A. ADJUSTING BARREL
F. LOCKNUT
REAR CABLE HANGER
B. CABLE ANCHOR BOLT
STIRRUP CABLE
G.
C. PIVOT BOLT
BRAKE ARM
BRAKE SHOE
BRAKE RUBBER
D.
CENTER-PULL BRAKE

C. PIVOT BOLTS
SPRING
ATTACHES TO FRAME HERE
CANTILEVER BRAKE

HAND BRAKES

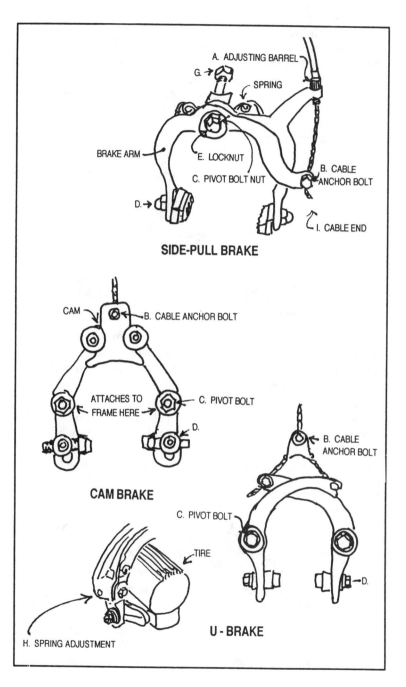

A. ADJUSTING BARREL

G.

SPRING

BRAKE ARM

E. LOCKNUT

C. PIVOT BOLT NUT

B. CABLE ANCHOR BOLT

D.

I. CABLE END

SIDE-PULL BRAKE

CAM

B. CABLE ANCHOR BOLT

ATTACHES TO FRAME HERE

C. PIVOT BOLT

D.

CAM BRAKE

B. CABLE ANCHOR BOLT

C. PIVOT BOLT

D.

TIRE

H. SPRING ADJUSTMENT

U - BRAKE

If that doesn't adjust the brakes enough, turn the adjusting barrel all the way down and then loosen the cable anchor bolt (B) at the end of the cable and adjust there. To tighten the cable at (B) you need three hands — a friend, a "third-hand tool," a clamp, or a piece of rope — to hold the brake pulled in tight while you pull the cable and tighten the nut.

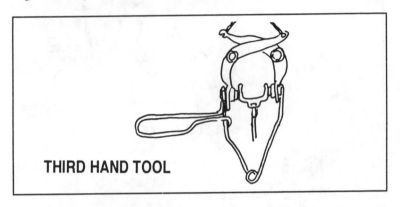

THIRD HAND TOOL

2) BRAKE RUBBERS (PADS) may be worn and need to be replaced or rotated. Sizes differ so make sure to get the right size (take the old one with you). Slide (or pry or pull) the old rubber out and slide the new one in. IMPORTANT — make sure that the open end of the brake shoe (the metal holder that the rubber fits into) is facing the rear of the bike. Otherwise the rubber can just be pushed out by the pressure of the wheel and you'll have no brakes. Many newer brake rubbers can't be removed from the shoes — replace shoe and rubber together.

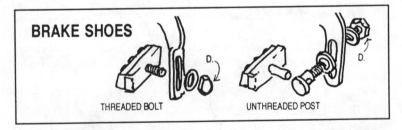

BRAKE SHOES

THREADED BOLT   UNTHREADED POST

3) BRAKE SHOES may not be at the right height. They should hit squarely on the wheel rim — not the tire (that will wear out the tire fast and can stop you dangerously fast).

Loosen nut (D) to adjust. Some brakes have an adjustment at (D) to change the angle of the brake shoe as well as the height.

4) WHEEL may not be centered or it may not be "true". That will cause the brake rubbers to hit unevenly. To center the wheel: loosen the axle nuts and hold the wheel centered in the frame as you re-tighten the axle nuts (see p. 28). To true the wheel, see p. 38.

5) BRAKES MAY NOT BE CENTERED. This will cause the brake to rub more on one side. Loosen nut (G) that holds the brake to the frame and straighten the brake. For cam and cantilever brakes, make sure the two pivot bolts are adjusted equally.

6) SPRING may not be centered (mainly on side-pull brakes). This causes one side to rub more. Loosen nut (G) on the pivot bolt and move the spring until the spring is even and pushes on both sides of the brake (brake arms) evenly. Re-tighten (G). You can also hit (gently!) the spring from above with a hammer and screwdriver to get it more centered (hit on the side that's farther from the rim).

On cam and cantilever brakes the springs are behind the pivot bolts (C) and go into a hole in the boss (the bump on the frame where the bolt attaches). For U-brakes, the springs are behind the pivot bolts (C) and adjust with the little allen bolt (H) on the side of the brake (see p. 51). Springs on both sides should have the same tension.

7) RIM may not be clean, which can cause uneven grabbing or squeaking. Squeaking itself doesn't hurt the bike. Make sure that the rim is free of dirt and oil. You can use alcohol to clean the rim — it won't hurt rubber like kerosene. The rim may have blips in it (see p. 29) which can cause grabbing.

8) BRAKE MAY BE LOOSE. This will cause jerky grabbing or shaking. Tighten nut (G) that holds the brake to the frame. Brake arms may also be loose. Tighten pivot bolt(s) (C). Don't get them too tight or the brake won't work. If you have two pivot bolts, they should be adjusted equally.

9) BRAKE CABLE may not be sliding easily through the cable casing, either because it's too big for the casing (or the casing is too small for it), the cable is catching on a kink in the casing or a burr at the end of the casing, a loop in the casing is too big, the cable is frayed, or it needs grease. If you can't grease the cable immediately, oil will do temporarily. You can usually drip oil into the casing without removing the cable. Or the brake cable may be broken. When buying a new cable, you need to know whether you need a ball end $\subset$━━ (most 10-speeds) or a barrel end (most mountain bikes and 3-speeds) $\subset$━━ . Look where the cable attaches to the lever. Cable lengths may differ also, get an exact replacement.

TO REPLACE THE BRAKE CABLE. Loosen the cable anchor bolt (B) and pull the cable out from the hand lever end. Note how it attaches to the lever. Push the new cable through, starting at the lever, greasing the cable lightly where it goes through casing. Check the casing for kinks or jagged ends. Clip off any jagged ends with a wire-cutter. Make sure the cable casings have the right curve, not straight and not too big a loop. Squeeze the hand lever several times — new cables stretch. Now go back to (1) (p. 49) and adjust the brakes. Be aware that since new cables stretch you may need to re-adjust fairly soon.

Cable ends are small plastic or metal caps that fit on the end of cables to help prevent unravelling (see p. 51). Use them.

10) BRAKE LEVER may be sticking — because of lack of oil or a bent part. Try oil first. Bent parts can often be straightened — carefully because metal bent too much can break.

11) BRAKES may be sticking. This can be due to a lack of oil, general funkiness, weak brake springs, pivot bolt(s) (C) too tight, or a bent part (like the brake arms). Try cleaning, or loosening the pivot bolt(s) slightly. On brakes that have 2 pivot bolts — one side too tight can cause one shoe to rub. Side-pull brakes sometimes have a screw at (C) or more often have both a nut and an acorn-shaped locknut. If you need to bend the brake arms (pry apart with a screwdriver or twist with a crescent wrench) — do so very gently. Don't break the arm. To take the brake apart, see p. 56.

12) TOE-IN may be wrong. To provide maximum efficiency and to prevent squealing, brake shoes should be "toed-in." This means that the front part of the brake pad should hit the rim first when you apply the brakes. This adjustment is very subtle. The front of the brake should only touch the wheel very slightly (.5mm!) before the rear. Use as little toe-in as possible, just enough to keep the brake from squealing. Some cantilever brakes have a way to adjust toe-in at nut (D), others have to be bent. If you must bend your brake, do it carefully, using a small (6") crescent wrench. Grasp the brake arm near the pad with the crescent wrench and twist slightly to toe-in the brake shoes. Be very careful not to strain the pivot bolt or break the arm.

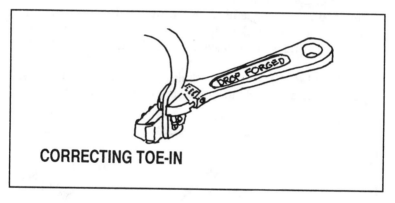

CORRECTING TOE-IN

13) BRAKE LEVER may be loose on the handlebars. If the nut or screw that holds the lever on is visible, just tighten it. If is isn't visible, it's inside the lever and you'll probably have to loosen and then push aside the cable to reach it. To loosen the cable, use the quick-release mechanism if you have one, unhook the short "stirrup cable," or loosen the cable anchor bolt (B) on the brake. Try to keep the cable from slipping all the way through the anchor bolt — it's sometimes hard to put back, especially if the end is frayed. With the cable out of the way, reach in with a screwdriver (or a socket or allen wrench for some brakes) and tighten the bolt. Re-connect the brake cable.

This is also the procedure if you want to change the location of the levers. Get them so they 're comfortable for you. Be careful

when you loosen the lever not to undo the bolt all the way —
it's hard to get back on. Just loosen a little and move the lever.

TAPED HANDLEBARS. With taped handlebars, you have to
undo the tape to move the levers. Pull out the handlebar end
plugs and unwind the tape. Plastic tape has no adhesive and
cloth has little. To rewind the tape, begin near the center of
the handlebars. Shove the extra tape in the end of the
handlebars and replace the end plug (see p. 43). Some people
prefer to tape in the other direction and hold the top end in
place with sticky tape.

OTHER HAND BRAKES. There are other, less common, types
of hand brakes: drum and disc brakes (the brake is in the hub,
similar to car brakes, and operated by hand levers), hydraulic
brakes (wheel rim brakes that use hydraulic fluid), and stirrup
brakes (rim brakes using a system of rods rather than cables).

TO TAKE BRAKES APART. Brakes get funky and can be taken
apart and cleaned. Hand brakes are easy, just watch how the
spring(s) fit.

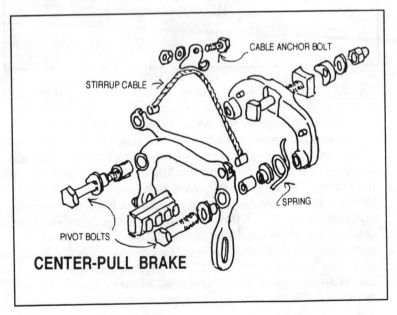

CABLE ANCHOR BOLT

STIRRUP CABLE →

SPRING

PIVOT BOLTS

CENTER-PULL BRAKE

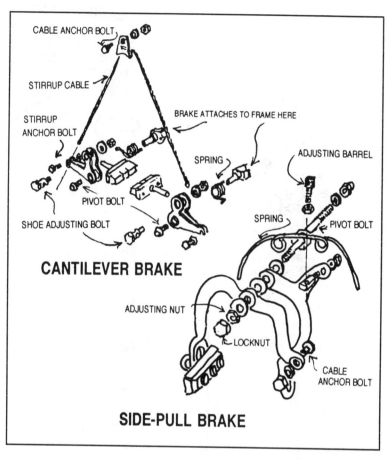

CABLE ANCHOR BOLT

STIRRUP CABLE

STIRRUP
ANCHOR BOLT

BRAKE ATTACHES TO FRAME HERE

SPRING

ADJUSTING BARREL

PIVOT BOLT

SPRING

PIVOT BOLT

SHOE ADJUSTING BOLT

CANTILEVER BRAKE

ADJUSTING NUT

LOCKNUT

CABLE
ANCHOR BOLT

SIDE-PULL BRAKE

COASTER BRAKES are more complicated but can be taken apart. Be sure you know what you are getting into before you attempt this. Brake models differ so I won't give details but there are diagrams of two common kinds on p. 58 to give you an idea of what is inside. Ask your local bike shop if they have a diagram for your particular brake. Take out the parts carefully and keep them in order. When you get the hub apart, check for worn bearings (A), cones (B), clutch (C), clutch spring (D), driver (E), and shoes or discs (F). Replace worn or broken parts and clean well. Sand the inside of the hub with emery paper to eliminate glaze and clean out the dust well. Grease well and re-assemble.

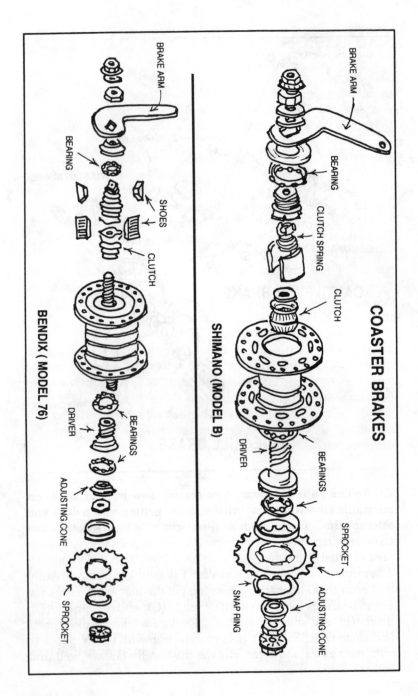

COASTER BRAKES

BRAKE ARM

BEARING

CLUTCH SPRING

CLUTCH

DRIVER

BEARINGS

SPROCKET

ADJUSTING CONE

SNAP RING

SHIMANO (MODEL B)

BRAKE ARM

BEARING

SHOES

CLUTCH

DRIVER

BEARINGS

ADJUSTING CONE

SPROCKET

BENDIX (MODEL 76)

GEARS: MULTI-SPEED

This section applies to all multi-speed bikes that rely on derailleurs and various size front and rear sprockets. Ten-speeds are the most common and for simplicity I'll refer to them, but this information will also apply to 5-24 speed bikes.

The principle of a multi-speed bike is to change the ratio of how often the pedals go around to how often the wheel turns by changing the size of the sprockets that the chain goes around. Ten-speeds have 2 sprockets on the front ("chainwheel") and 5 on the rear hub ("freewheel"). That gives you 10 combinations. Five-speeds have only one chainwheel in front; 15 or more speeds have a triple chainwheel. Freewheels can come with up to eight sprockets so other gear combinations are also possible. More gears are not necessarily better and can create problems. The range of gear ratios is often more important than the number of gears. Beware of hype and fads.

There is a **derailleur** (which comes from the French word for "to unrail") both front and rear that moves the chain from one sprocket to another. There are adjustments to control how far in each direction the derailleur moves so that the derailleur moves the chain to all sprockets but not off either end. The rear derailleur also takes up slack in the chain to compensate for different sprocket sizes.

HOW TO USE THE GEARS. As you've certainly discovered, it's harder to pedal going uphill than downhill or on level ground. Harder pedaling means more strain on your legs and slower pedaling. A choice of gears allows you to equalize the effort.

Your body works best when you are pedalling at least 60 rpms (revolutions per minute), which is one revolution per second. This is a healthy tempo for your knees, it helps pump blood from your legs to your heart, and it helps keep your muscles supple. The idea behind having all those gears is so that you can always keep your feet moving at that tempo, no matter how fast the bike is going.

59

SHIFTING GEARS. You shift gears by moving the shift levers mounted on the frame or handlebars. Shift gears while you're pedaling, but not pedaling hard. DO NOT shift while you're freewheeling (coasting) or standing still. If the freewheel isn't turning, too much strain is placed on the cable and/or derailleur. The derailleur can't move the chain to the next sprocket if the sprockets aren't turning — and pedaling makes them turn.

There are two principle types of shift levers: friction and indexed shifters and each can be mounted in various places.

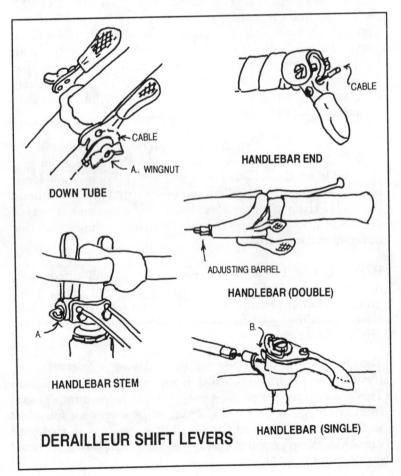

CABLE

HANDLEBAR END

CABLE

A.. WINGNUT

DOWN TUBE

ADJUSTING BARREL

HANDLEBAR (DOUBLE)

A.

HANDLEBAR STEM

B.

DERAILLEUR SHIFT LEVERS

HANDLEBAR (SINGLE)

FRICTION LEVERS. There are no fixed positions to tell you when the bike is in gear as on a 3-speed. As you move the lever, the derailleur moves the chain from one sprocket to the next. You soon learn to hear and feel when you are in gear — it scrapes, chatters, crunches, and rubs otherwise. Don't panic if that happens — just move the lever a little. But don't let the noise continue.

INDEXED SHIFT LEVERS. These are a more recent innovation where the levers click as they shift in increments. On some models, gears are marked on the levers. All parts of this system must match — levers, derailleurs, and freewheel — and they also use special thicker gear cables. Don't try to change just one part. Many of these levers also have a setting (B) (see p. 60) so they can work as friction levers. This is especially useful if the gears get out of adjustment — you can switch to the friction setting until you can re-adjust the whole system.

ADJUSTING FRICTION SHIFT LEVERS. There should be an adjustment (A) on the shift lever — sometimes just a screw, sometimes a wing nut you can turn by hand (far better). This controls how easily the shift lever shifts. It should be loose enough to shift easily but if it's too loose the lever won't hold in place and the bike won't stay in gear. This may need adjusting often, even as you ride.

TO REMOVE SHIFT LEVERS. With the gears in position so there is no tension on the cables (small freewheel sprocket and usually the small chainwheel sprocket), simply undo the bolt holding the levers on the frame or handlebars.

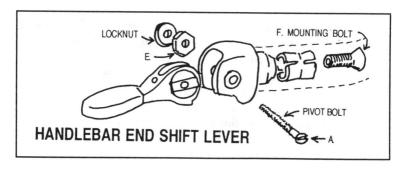

LOCKNUT   F. MOUNTING BOLT

E →

PIVOT BOLT

HANDLEBAR END SHIFT LEVER   ← A

For **handlebar end shifters** you have to remove the lever itself, bolt (E) before you can get at the bolt (F) (use allen wrench) that holds the assembly in place. You may also have to remove the handlebar tape to get at the cable housing that runs either through the handlebars or under the tape.

TO REPLACE GEAR CABLE. Undo the cable anchor bolt (C) on the derailleur, pull the cable out and unhook it from the shift lever (you may have to undo (A) on the shift lever and remove the lever to get the cable out). Put the new cable through. Make sure to get one with the same kind of end and same thickness as the old one. Remember to grease the new cable where it goes through the casing. Check cable casings for kinks or burrs (jagged edges) and proper curves. Where the casing curves, the curve should be gentle — not too big and not too little. If a cable ever breaks near an anchor bolt , you can often do a temporary emergency repair by shortening the casing a little which will have the effect of lengthening the cable. Cable ends, little plastic or metal caps, fit on the end of the cable and help prevent unravelling.

TO ADJUST THE CABLE. Loosen the cable anchor bolt (C) on the derailleur and pull the cable so there is no slack (with the lever so the cable is loosest). Tighten the cable anchor bolt. If the cable is too loose, the derailleur won't go on the large sprocket. If the cable is too tight, it won't go back to the small sprocket. Careful with cable anchor bolts, they are small and break easily — tighten gently. New cables may stretch for a while and you'll have to do this adjustment several times with a new bike or cable. You may need to re-adjust the derailleur after adjusting the cable.

ADJUSTING DERAILLEURS. There are several makes of derailleurs, each with many models. They will all need to be adjusted and can be adjusted easily. The places to adjust vary on different makes and models but if you know the principle you should be able to find the adjusting screws. I'll explain one model in detail and give diagrams of others. It's easier to adjust derailleurs with the bike on a rack or upside down (careful not to rest the bike on the cables) so you can pedal and shift gears to test the adjustments.

FRONT DERAILLEUR: (H) controls the derailleur's position on the frame. The derailleur cage should be parallel to the chainwheel and should clear the large chainwheel by about 1/4". With the cage over the small chainwheel, adjust the cable tension (C) so that there is no slack. Adjust (D) so that the chain goes easily on to the large derailleur without going so far that it goes off on the outside. Shift (turning the pedals as you shift) so the derailleur cage is over the small chainwheel. Screw (E) adjusts the derailleur in this position. You want it so the chain goes down to the small chainwheel but not off completely.

If the chain falls off the chainwheel while you're riding, it usually means the front derailleur is out of adjustment (or you have a bent tooth on the chainwheel, see p. 83). If the derailleur is the problem, adjust (E) if it comes off inside and (D) if it comes off outside. If you need to free the chain from the cage, loosen nut (I).

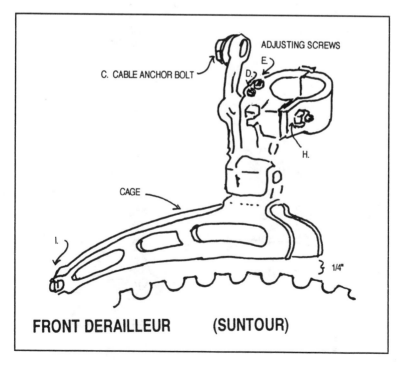

FRONT DERAILLEUR   **(SUNTOUR)**

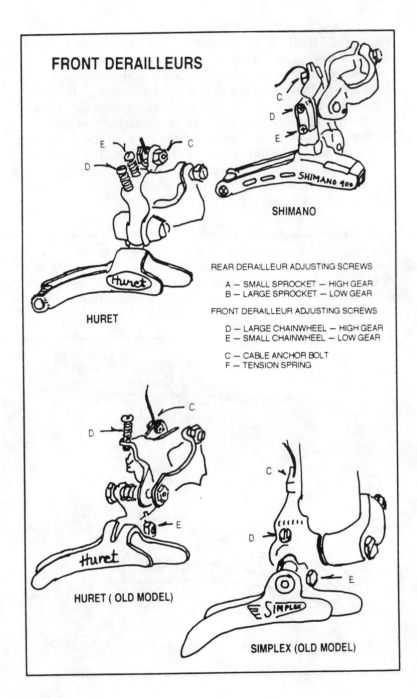

FRONT DERAILLEURS

SHIMANO

HURET

REAR DERAILLEUR ADJUSTING SCREWS

A — SMALL SPROCKET — HIGH GEAR
B — LARGE SPROCKET — LOW GEAR

FRONT DERAILLEUR ADJUSTING SCREWS

D — LARGE CHAINWHEEL — HIGH GEAR
E — SMALL CHAINWHEEL — LOW GEAR

C — CABLE ANCHOR BOLT
F — TENSION SPRING

HURET (OLD MODEL)

SIMPLEX (OLD MODEL)

64

REAR DERAILLEURS

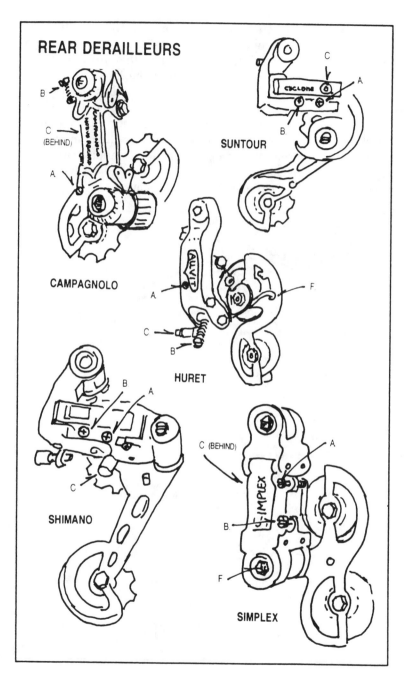

CAMPAGNOLO

SUNTOUR

HURET

SHIMANO

SIMPLEX

REAR DERAILLEUR: Shift the lever (remember to turn the pedals as you shift) so the cable is loosest and adjust (C) so that there is no slack. With the shift lever in this position, adjust (A) so the derailleur is centered over the small freewheel sprocket. Move the shift lever (turning the pedals as you shift) so the cable is as tight as possible and adjust (B) so the derailleur is centered over the large sprocket. Shift the gears back and forth a few times to see if the derailleur moves the chain easily onto all the sprockets. If not, re-adjust either (A) or (B). With the chain on the small sprocket, adjust (G) so the derailleur body is parallel to the chain stay.

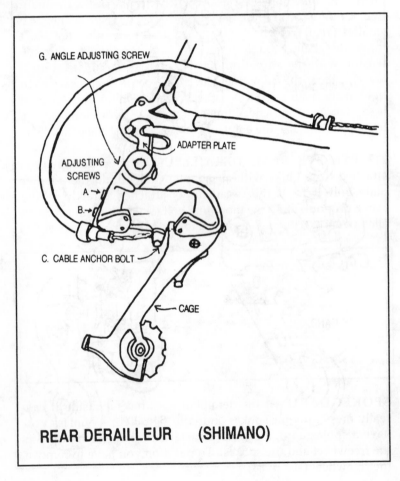

REAR DERAILLEUR   (SHIMANO)

TO ADJUST INDEXED GEAR SYSTEM. If you have a "friction" mode at (B) (see p. 60) on your indexed shift levers, you can use that to do the major derailleur adjustments.

Put the bike in the highest gear (big chainwheel sprocket, small freewheel sprocket) and adjust as you would for friction-type levers (see p. 63 & 66). Then put the bike in the lowest gear (small chainwheel sprocket, large freewheel sprocket) and adjust as you would for friction levers.

Then, with bike in highest gear, switch into the index mode for fine tuning. Shift the freewheel to the next gear (next to smallest rear freewheel sprocket). If the derailleur doesn't move the chain enough or moves it too far, adjust the cable tension with the **adjusting barrel** (on rear derailleur or shift lever). Turn the adjusting barrel out counter-clockwise to tighten the cable. Do this same procedure with each gear in turn. Go back and check them all again. If you don't have a friction setting, use the adjusting barrel to adjust the gears.

TO REMOVE REAR DERAILLEUR. If your derailleur is attached to the bike with an adapter plate, undo the adapter plate bolt (H). If the derailleur is attached directly to the frame dropout, undo the mounting bolt (I) which often needs an allen wrench. You may also need to undo the chain (see p. 88)

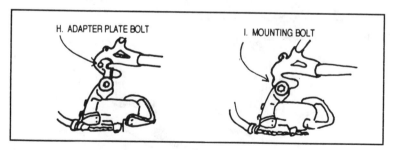

SPOKEGUARD. If the derailleur goes too far inside it can really mess up your spokes and your derailleur — unless you have a spokeguard, a plastic or metal disc that fits in between the freewheel and the spokes. To put it on you have to remove the freewheel (see p. 84).

DERAILLEUR GUARD. You can also get a metal guard to put over your derailleur to help protect it.

DERAILLEUR OVERHAUL. People often think derailleurs are broken or useless when they aren't. The derailleur may be out of adjustment or it may be so dirty and sticky that it no longer works. Or just one part may be bent or broken. Look carefully. What is wrong? Out of alignment? The rear cage should be parallel to the chain stay. A part bent? Straighten it (take the derailleur apart if you need to). Little wheels don't turn easily? Whole derailleur sticky? Try lubricant. Or take the whole thing apart and clean it well. Check adjusting screws (A and B) and cable tension (C) (see p. 66). Derailleurs have different ways to adjust the chain tension, often near the tension spring (F) (the spring where the cage attaches to the body of the derailleur). This will change the amount of tension on the derailleur cage and thus the amount of slack in the chain that the derailleur will take up.

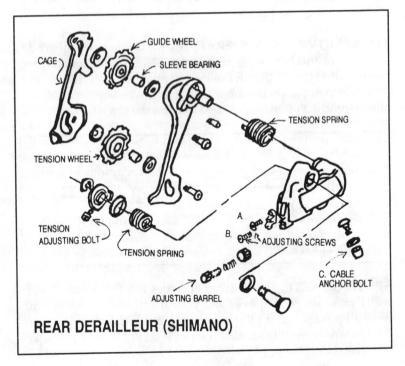

REAR DERAILLEUR (SHIMANO)

GEAR RATIOS. The ratio of the gears (how often the wheel turns compared to how often the pedals turn) on a 10-speed depends on the number of teeth on both the freewheel and the chainwheel sprockets. The formula for finding the ratio for any gear is to multiply the diameter (in inches) of the rear wheel (i.e. 27) by the number of teeth on the chainwheel ("front") and divide by the number of teeth on the freewheel sprocket ("rear").

For example, with 36 and 50 teeth on the chainwheel and 14, 17, 20, 24, 28 teeth on the freewheel (27" wheel), the gear ratios are:

gear	front	rear	ratio	gear	front	rear	ratio
1	36	28	34.7	6	50	28	48.2
2	36	24	40.5	7	50	24	56.3
3	36	20	48.6	8	50	20	67.5
4	36	17	57.2	9	50	17	79.4
5	36	14	69.4	10	50	14	96.4

For first gear that's 27 times 36, then divide by 28, and the result is 34.7. This means that in the first gear you go 34.7 x π inches (remember your math, π=3.1414) or 109" for every revolution of the pedals. Notice the overlap. Low numbers in the ratio column are good for climbing hills with less effort, high numbers mean more distance covered per pedal revolution. The more difference between high and low, the greater variety you have in your gears. The range is often more important than the number of different gears. The closer the numbers are, the more subtle variations you have (used largely for racing).

CHANGING GEAR COMPONENTS. You may want to get a different chainwheel and/or freewheel to get a better gear ratio. Be very careful doing this because if you change the gear ratio you may also need to change the length of the chain (simple, see p. 88) and maybe also your derailleur (also simple, see p. 67). Some derailleurs can't handle wide ratios (can't take up enough slack in the chain) so keep that in mind if you're changing things. Changing gear components is tricky — ask at the bike shop where you buy your parts.

GEARS: 3 SPEED

Three-speed gears are located inside the rear wheel hub. There is a **trigger** on the handlebar (usually Sturmey-Archer) or a **handgrip** (Shimano or Sturmey-Archer) that turns with three places where it catches. Pulling the trigger or turning the handgrip pulls the cable tighter (or loosens it) which changes the gears inside the rear wheel hub. If the cable isn't adjusted to the proper length, the gears won't work right — the pedals may turn without engaging or the bike may not have all three gears. There is an "**adjusting barrel**" (B) where the cable attaches to the indicator or indicator chain near the hub.

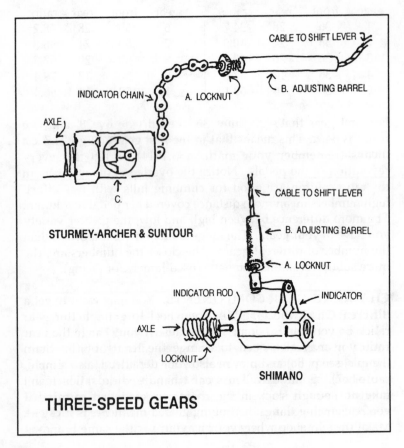

CABLE TO SHIFT LEVER

INDICATOR CHAIN

A. LOCKNUT

B. ADJUSTING BARREL

AXLE

C.

STURMEY-ARCHER & SUNTOUR

CABLE TO SHIFT LEVER

B. ADJUSTING BARREL

A. LOCKNUT

INDICATOR ROD

INDICATOR

AXLE

LOCKNUT

SHIMANO

THREE-SPEED GEARS

TO ADJUST. Put the bike in middle gear. Loosen locknut (A). For Sturmey-Archer or Suntour gears, turn the adjusting barrel (B) so that the point (C) where the indicator chain becomes a rod is even with the end of the axle (look through the hole in the nut). For Shimano gears the pointer should point to the mark on the indicator, or "N" should be visible through the hole in the indicator. Remember, this is in middle gear.

You might not be able to adjust the cable enough by this method. If not, there are other places to adjust it. Some cables have a place to adjust right before you get to the adjusting barrel. Loosen nut (D) and adjust so there is no slack (but not so it is tight) in the loosest gear. Now do the first adjustment above.

If you don't have that adjustment, follow the cable from the handlebars down toward the rear hub. Find the "fulcrum" where the covered cable ends and the plain wire begins. Loosen nut (E) and move the fulcrum along the frame, toward the front of the bike if the cable was too loose, toward the back if it was too tight. Get it so there is no slack in the loosest gear. Tighten (E). Now do the first adjustment above (with the adjusting barrel).

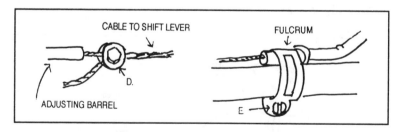

SIMPLE GEAR PROBLEMS. There are some simple things to check on your gears before you consider taking the hub apart. **Indicator chains** sometimes aren't screwed in tight or are bent, the **cable** may be frayed or need grease (oil will do in a pinch), **cable housing** may have kinks or burrs (jagged ends) which will prevent the cable from sliding smoothly, **gear levers** sometimes need oil, or the gear in the hub may need **oil** (it needs it often). Make sure your gear trigger or handgrip is the same brand as the hub — otherwise you might not be able to adjust the gears correctly.

LUBRICATION. There will generally be an oil fitting on the hub. Lubricate often (once a month) with heavy oil.

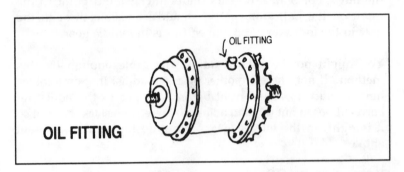

OIL FITTING

TO REPLACE A CABLE. Cables break (or sometimes rust) and need to be replaced. Undo the adjusting barrel (B) near the hub and pull out the cable. For a **trigger** on the handlebar, push the loose cable forward until it can be unhooked from the trigger and pull it out. Notice how it goes so you can put the new one through. For a **handgrip**, you have to take the handgrip apart (one or two screws). Be careful not to lose the little ball bearing inside (it's what makes the gears catch). Grease the new cable as you put it in place.

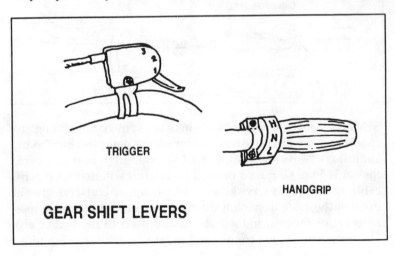

TRIGGER

HANDGRIP

GEAR SHIFT LEVERS

TO REPLACE INDICATOR. The indicator chain or indicator rod can be replaced easily if it's rusty or bent. Just unscrew the gear cable from the chain or rod and then unscrew the chain or rod from the hub. Get an exact replacement. Screw it back in hand tight and re-attach and adjust the cable (see p. 71). If you don't move the locknut, you may be able to avoid re-adjusting the gears after you put in the new indicator chain or rod.

SPROCKET REMOVAL. The rear sprocket is held on by a strong circular spring clip. To remove the sprocket, simply pry off the clip with a screwdriver. If the sprocket is dished (not symmetrical), notice which side goes out. You can change your sprocket size if you want — the relationship of the three gears will remain the same but all will be higher or lower depending on whether you get a larger or smaller sprocket.

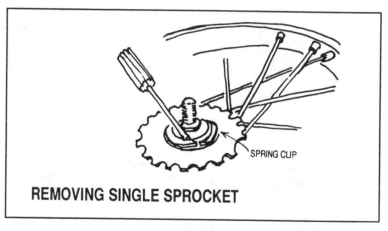

SPRING CLIP

REMOVING SINGLE SPROCKET

HUB OVERHAUL. Three-speed hubs have many, many little parts inside. You can take them apart but do so very carefully (or let a professional mechanic do it). If you're not intimidated by the diagrams on page 74 and you decide to take the hub apart, check for worn bearings (A), cones (B), gear pawls (C), pawl springs (D), gear teeth (E), clutch (F), clutch spring (G), sliding key (H), or bent axle or dust caps. Replace any worn parts and clean all parts well. Adjust the cones carefully when you re-assemble. Oil all the inside parts well, through oil fitting (K).

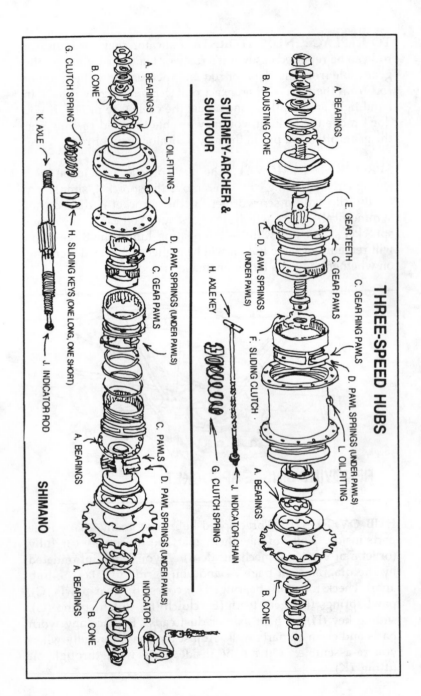

THREE-SPEED HUBS

STURMEY-ARCHER & SUNTOUR

A. BEARINGS
B. ADJUSTING CONE
E. GEAR TEETH
C. GEAR RING PAWLS
C. GEAR PAWLS
D. PAWL SPRINGS (UNDER PAWLS)
F. SLIDING CLUTCH
D. PAWL SPRINGS (UNDER PAWLS)
L. OIL FITTING
A. BEARINGS
B. CONE
G. CLUTCH SPRING
J. INDICATOR CHAIN

SHIMANO

G. CLUTCH SPRING
B. CONE
A. BEARINGS
L. OIL FITTING
D. PAWL SPRINGS (UNDER PAWLS)
C. GEAR PAWLS
H. AXLE KEY
C. GEAR PAWLS
D. PAWL SPRINGS (UNDER PAWLS)
A. BEARINGS
C. PAWLS
D. PAWL SPRINGS (UNDER PAWLS)
A. BEARINGS
B. CONE
INDICATOR
K. AXLE
H. SLIDING KEYS (ONE LONG, ONE SHORT)
J. INDICATOR ROD

PEDALS

Pedals screw into the crank. Right and left pedals have different threads and aren't interchangeable. The right pedal has normal right-hand thread but the left pedal has left-hand thread that screws in counter-clockwise. This is so the natural pedaling motion doesn't unscrew the pedal. Pedals should be on very tight, otherwise the threads get stripped and you may have to get a whole new crank. A regular wrench may not fit the space between the pedal and the crank and you'll need a special thin pedal wrench. If you need new pedals, get the right size for your crank (axle diameter and threads differ).

Most pedals have bearings inside which need to be taken apart and greased occasionally. Some pedals are made so they can't be taken apart.

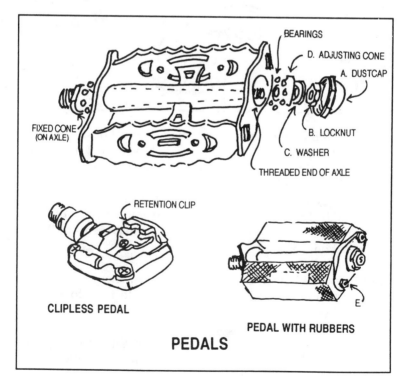

BEARINGS
D. ADJUSTING CONE
A. DUSTCAP
FIXED CONE
(ON AXLE)
B. LOCKNUT
C. WASHER
THREADED END OF AXLE

RETENTION CLIP

CLIPLESS PEDAL

PEDAL WITH RUBBERS

E

PEDALS

TO TAKE PEDAL APART. If you have a removeable dust-cap (A), unscrew it or pry it off. Remove locknut (B), lockwasher (C), and adjusting cone (D). If you don't have a removeable dust-cap you may have to take off the two pedal rubbers (nut E) to reach the locknut and adjusting cone.

Pedals are an exception to the general rule that bearings come in matched sets. Because the pedal axle is tapered, the two sets of bearings may have different amounts of balls. Take your pedal apart carefully and count the balls. Write it down. Clean and re-assemble.

TO ADJUST PEDAL. Screw in the adjusting cone so that the pedal turns freely but without extra play. Tighten locknut. Test it again, Replace the dust-cap.

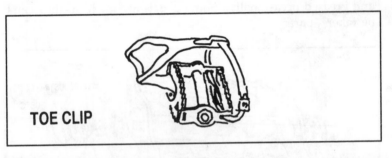

TOE CLIP

TOE CLIPS really help when riding. They bolt to the "rat-trap" pedals found on 10-speeds and hold your foot in place on the pedal so that you can pull up and push around when you pedal. You can adjust the strap (and bend the toe clip itself on metal ones) to change how tightly the toe clip holds your foot. It should be looser for city riding where you have lots of stops. Toe clips come in different sizes — get one that keeps the ball of your foot on the pedal.

CLIPLESS PEDALS. These require special shoes (with cleats attached to them) and are designed to hold your foot to the pedal without toe clips. The cleats hook on to a retention clip on the pedal (see p. 75). Old style cleats protruded from the shoe; newer ones are recessed. The retention clip can be adjusted to make it easier or harder to remove your foot from the pedal.

CRANK

KINDS OF CRANKS. There are three main kinds of cranks. Some bikes (primarily single speeds) have **"one-piece"** cranks where the crank and bottom bracket axle are one continuous piece. To remove these see p. 82. On most bikes the cranks come off the bottom bracket (also called the hanger) axle or spindle. Some cranks attach to the bottom bracket axle by **cotter keys** (also called cotter pins) (see p. 78) but most bikes now use a **"cotterless"** system .

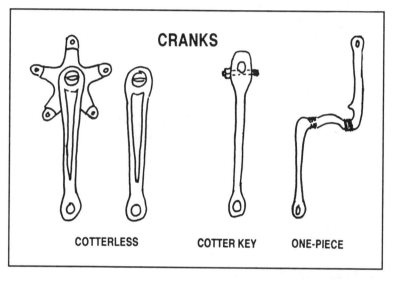

CRANKS

COTTERLESS   **COTTER KEY**   **ONE-PIECE**

The chainwheel can usually be removed from the right crank (see p. 83). Threads in the crank for the pedal differ (p. 75).

COTTERLESS CRANKS need special tools. Remove the dustcap (A) with a screwdriver or hex wrench. Undo the fixing bolt (B) with the socket wrench part of the crank puller (step 1). Then screw the threaded part of the crank puller into the dustcap threads in the crank (with the bolt on the crank puller screwed out) (step 2). Slowly tighten the bolt (clockwise) on the crank puller, which will push the crank off the hanger axle. Be gentle, it may be on very tight.

To replace the crank, put the crank on the axle. Make sure the crank is facing the right way — opposite from the other crank. Put the fixing bolt (B) on the end of the axle and tighten slowly, wiggling the crank as you go to get it snug. Replace the dust-cap. Make sure this bolt stays tight — check it regularly.

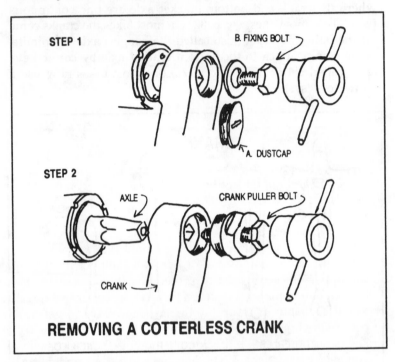

REMOVING A COTTERLESS CRANK

COTTER KEY CRANKS. To remove a crank held on by cotter keys, undo the crank cotter key nut (A) and remove the washer (B). Then you want to bang out the cotter key with a hammer — but without damaging it or the bottom bracket bearings, which is tricky. Place a piece of wood over the threaded end of the cotter key (or use a punch) so as not to damage the threads. If you damage them the nut won't go back on and you'll need a new cotter key. If you have enough room to leave the nut on (but loose enough so the cotter key can move) do so. Then after the first gentle blow with the hammer to loosen the cotter key, you can take the nut off. If any threads did get slightly damaged, the nut will probably straighten them up.

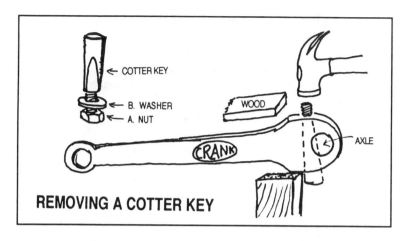

COTTER KEY

B. WASHER

A. NUT

WOOD

CRANK

AXLE

REMOVING A COTTER KEY

IMPORTANT. When you hammer on the crank, rest the crank on a piece of wood or metal so the crank gets knocked against the wood and not the bottom bracket bearings. You don't want to damage those bottom bracket bearings!

Cotter keys are almost always hard to get out. They are usually in very tight. Try squirting Liquid Wrench (and tap the cotter key so it gets inside). If you still can't get it off, forget the upper block of wood to protect the threads (keeping the bottom one in place) and smash (gently) the cotter key directly. You'll probably mess up the threads (and have to get a new cotter key) but you'll also probably get it out. Once the cotter key is out, the crank will slide off the bottom bracket axle. If you get a new cotter key, you may have to file or grind down the flat part to get a good fit and have enough room for the nut to go on.

TO REPLACE CRANK with cotter key. Put the crank on the bottom bracket axle so the crank is flush with the end of the axle and so the flat part of the axle is lined up with the hole in the crank. Put the cotter key in place. With the block of wood under the crank, tap the cotter key in until it is tight and there is no play between the crank and axle (try wiggling the crank while holding the axle steady, preferably with the other crank). Put on the washer and nut (not too tight, small nuts strip easily).

79

Cotter keys come in different sizes — take your old one to get an exact replacement.

TO ADJUST CRANK with cotter key. If there is play between the crank and the bottom bracket axle (hold one crank in each hand and try to turn in opposite directions to find play), hammer the cotter key in more, wiggling the crank as you do this to seat the cotter key well (remember to rest the crank on a block of wood) and tighten the nut. DO NOT try to pull a cotter key through by tightening the nut — it will strip and you'll just have to replace it.

BENT CRANK. If your crank is bent, remove the pedal and slip a piece of pipe (with a diameter just big enough to fit over the crank) over the end of the crank up to the bend. Wrap a rag around the crank first to protect it if you want. Pull the pipe (and thus the crank) out gently. Be very careful. This is not the "authorized" method but it can work. Bike shops have special tools for this — or you may need to replace the crank.

BOTTOM BRACKET

The cranks attach to the bottom bracket axle, also called the **hanger** axle or **spindle**.

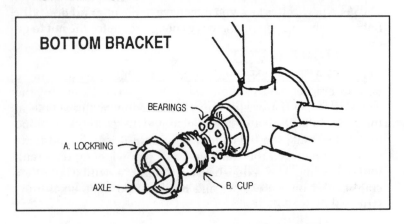

BOTTOM BRACKET

BEARINGS

A. LOCKRING

AXLE

B. CUP

TO REMOVE BOTTOM BRACKET. Cranks should be off, except with "one-piece" cranks. Loosen lockring or locknut (A) on the left side (use a wrench, vise grips, hammer and screwdriver, channel-lock pliers, or special lockring wrench), then undo the bottom bracket cup (B) (pin wrench or hammer and punch). That should expose the bearings on one side. If you have balls, count them — and be careful that they don't roll away. Pull out the axle and you'll be able to reach the bearings on the right side. There is usually no need to undo the right bottom bracket cup, it's meant to remain in place — but if you do (e.g. to replace races), it may have left-hand thread and unscrew clockwise.

Check bearings and races (cups and cones on axle) for wear; then clean, grease, and re-assemble. Install a bottom bracket **sleeve** (a piece of plastic or metal that fits inside the bottom bracket to keep dirt from falling down inside) if you don't already have one. When you replace the axle, make sure the long end is on the chainwheel side.

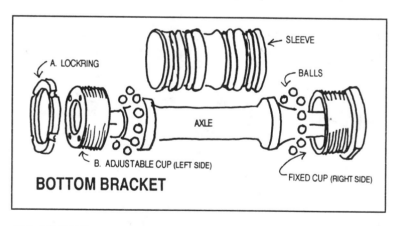

A. LOCKRING
SLEEVE
BALLS
AXLE
B. ADJUSTABLE CUP (LEFT SIDE)
FIXED CUP (RIGHT SIDE)
BOTTOM BRACKET

TO ADJUST BOTTOM BRACKET. Turn bottom bracket cup (B) until the axle rotates freely but without extra play. Tighten lockring (A) and check again.

SEALED BOTTOM BRACKET. These have cartridge bearings and the axle built into one sealed unit (see p. 82). Most can be removed by taking off the lockring (A)

81

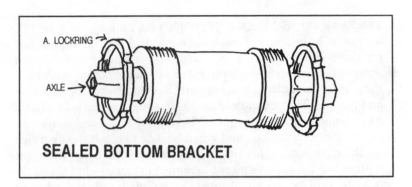

SEALED BOTTOM BRACKET

A. LOCKRING

AXLE

"ONE-PIECE" CRANK. If you have one of these, also called an Ashtabula crank, begin by removing the left pedal (left-hand thread, so unscrew clockwise). Then undo the locknut (A) (careful, this will also have left-hand thread), lockwasher (B), and adjusting cone (C) and pull everything else out from the right side. The bearings will usually be in retainers to make things easier.

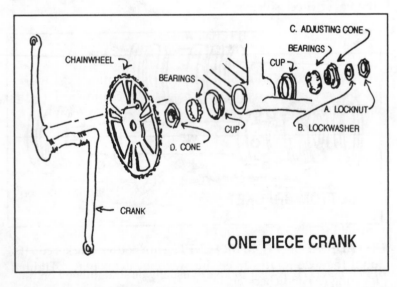

C. ADJUSTING CONE

BEARINGS

CUP

CHAINWHEEL

BEARINGS

A. LOCKNUT

B. LOCKWASHER

CUP

D. CONE

CRANK

ONE PIECE CRANK

If you need to remove the chainwheel, the right cone (D) unscrews from the crank and you can then slip the chainwheel off. The cups can be pushed out of the bottom bracket with a hammer and screwdriver, if necessary (see p.45).

CHAINWHEEL

TO REMOVE THE CHAINWHEEL. On 3-speed bikes the chainwheel is permanently attached to the right crank. For one-piece cranks, see p. 82. On 10-speeds the chainwheel can usually be removed from the crank by undoing 3-5 little bolts. Many double chainwheels can be taken further apart (more little bolts) so you can replace only one of the chainwheels if you want. You may want to change the size of your chainwheel sprockets to change your gear ratio (see p. 69).

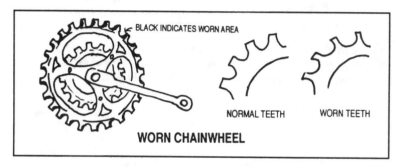

BLACK INDICATES WORN AREA

NORMAL TEETH   WORN TEETH

WORN CHAINWHEEL

WORN CHAINWHEELS. Chainwheels sometimes get worn out and need to be replaced. Look at the chainwheel teeth carefully for signs of wear.

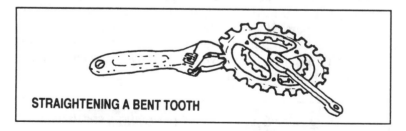

STRAIGHTENING A BENT TOOTH

BENT TOOTH. A bent tooth can usually be straightened on the bike — try a crescent wrench or vise grips. Be gentle.

ALIGNMENT. The chainwheel and freewheel must be lined up correctly. For 1 and 3-speeds, the chainwheel and rear sprocket should line up. For a 10-speed, looking from above, the middle

83

sprocket on the freewheel should line up between the two chainwheel sprockets. For other multiple gear bikes, the center of the front sprockets should line up with the center of the rear sprockets.

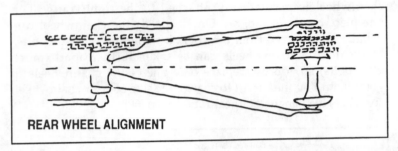

REAR WHEEL ALIGNMENT

You can correct alignment by placing a washer or shim (thin washer) on the appropriate side of the freewheel or getting a different length axle to change the chainwheel's position. You might also be able to move the right crank (and chainwheel) over some on the axle you have.

FREEWHEEL

Freewheels need to be removed to replace spokes on that side of the hub, to be replaced when worn (littlest gears wear fast), or to be taken apart. If you are taking a wheel completely apart, it's much easier to remove the freewheel before cutting the spokes. It's also best to remove the freewheel to clean it, unless yours is very hard to get off.

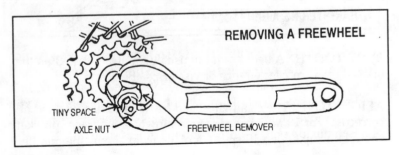

REMOVING A FREEWHEEL

TINY SPACE

AXLE NUT   FREEWHEEL REMOVER

TO REMOVE FREEWHEEL. Remove the wheel, remove the axle nut and washer on the freewheel side, put on a freewheel remover (get one that fits your kind of freewheel), and replace the axle nut loosely after the freewheel remover to hold it in place (leave a tiny space between them so the freewheel has room to loosen).

Turn the freewheel remover counter-clockwise. Freewheels are usually very hard to get off because every time you push the pedal you're tightening it more. Try Liquid Wrench (but be very careful not to get it <u>inside</u> the freewheel or you'll need to clean it and re-oil). Use a tight-fitting wrench with a long handle on the freewheel remover to get more leverage — or hold the remover stationary in a vise and turn the wheel (this gives you good leverage). Be careful not to damage the freewheel if the remover slips (removers also tend to strip easily). Be extra careful with the 2-pronged remover because often when the freewheel seems to be moving, it's only the remover and it's stripping something. The splined kind of freewheel is much easier to get a good hold on. Once the freewheel is loosened, remove the axle nut and keep unscrewing the freewheel. Save any shims or spacers you find behind the freewheel.

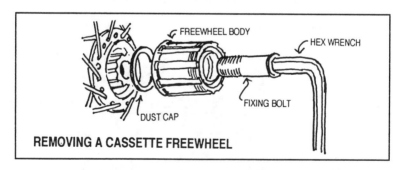

REMOVING A CASSETTE FREEWHEEL

CASSETTE TYPE FREEWHEEL. To remove this type (which fits on a special hub called a freehub), first remove the wheel axle. Then use an allen wrench to loosen freewheel fixing bolt and remove freewheel. These are lubricated from behind so you must remove them first. The sprockets are easy to remove. Loosen the top one (see p. 87) and the others slide off.

SPOKEGUARD. When the freewheel is off is a good time to put on a spokeguard, a plastic or metal disc that fits between the freewheel and the wheel and stops the derailleur from going over into the spokes and messing up both the spokes and the derailleur. Just put it on before replacing the freewheel; the freewheel holds it in place.

TO REPLACE FREEWHEEL. Just put it on hand tight — it will tighten itself as you pedal (which is why it gets so tight). Put a little grease or Never-Seez on the threads to make the freewheel easier to remove the next time. For cassette type freewheel, replace fixing bolt and wheel axle.

TO CLEAN FREEWHEEL. Freewheel can be on the wheel (except cassette type) although you run a great danger of getting kerosene in the hub that way (no problem if you're also planning to take the hub apart). Be careful not to get kerosene on the tires either. Squirt kerosene so it gets inside the freewheel. Spin the freewheel and watch the dirty kerosene come out. Add some more kerosene and spin again. When the kerosene starts coming out clean, You're done. Let it dry well (spin to help it and then leave it overnight). Then oil. Just run a light oil through until it starts coming out clean (omitting the kerosene step and using only oil will also work).

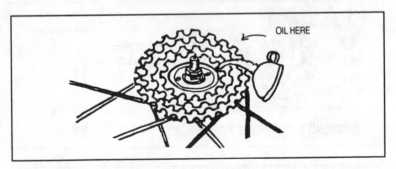
OIL HERE

TO TAKE FREEWHEEL APART. The freewheel can be taken further apart. Individual sprockets (or cogs) can be replaced. You'll probably need a chain whip for this but perhaps you can improvise with an old chain and a vise. Freewheels differ — find out how your particular freewheel is put together.

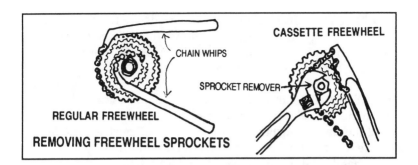

REMOVING FREEWHEEL SPROCKETS

CASSETTE FREEWHEEL

CHAIN WHIPS

SPROCKET REMOVER

REGULAR FREEWHEEL

You can also take the body of the freewheel apart but be careful not to lose the tiny balls and ratchet springs inside.

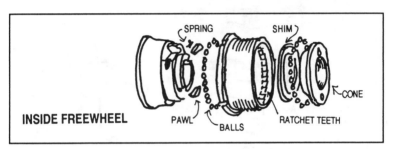

INSIDE FREEWHEEL

SPRING   SHIM

PAWL   BALLS   RATCHET TEETH   CONE

CHAIN

MASTER LINK. Chains on 1 and 3-speed bikes usually have a "master link" to make it easier to take the chain off. It'll look different from the others. Find it. Some snap off (pry with a screwdriver), some slide sideways, and some unscrew. When you replace the master link make sure the removeable part faces out.

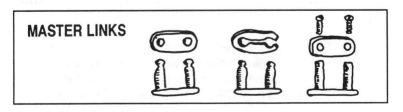

MASTER LINKS

NO MASTER LINK. Chains on 10-speeds are too thin to have room for a master link (they are thinner than 3-speed chains) so you just have to take out one of the rivets (it doesn't matter which). You'll need a chain tool to do this.

TO REMOVE A LINK. Put the chain tool in position (A). Turn the handle (making sure the pin hits squarely on the rivet) until the rivet is pushed <u>almost</u> out. DON'T push it completely out, leave it in the last part of the link. Otherwise you'll need three hands and much patience to get it back in.

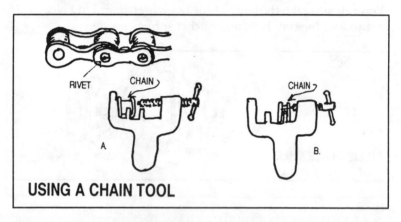

USING A CHAIN TOOL

TO RE-CONNECT THE CHAIN. Place the chain in position (A) and push the rivet back in. If the rivet came all the way out before, try holding it in place with needle-nose (thin) pliers while a friend turns the chain tool handle. Then check for a tight link (see below).

CHAIN LENGTH depends on your gear ratio. For 10-speeds the chain has to be long enough for the derailleur to work with the chain on both large sprockets. If the chain is too long or if the derailleur can't take up enough slack, the chain will slip, especially when on the small sprocket and under strain.

TIGHT LINK. A tight link can cause the chain to come off. Feel for tight links. On a 10-speed you can usually see them as the chain goes around the little derailleur wheels (the chain won't bend between those links). To loosen a tight link, bend the chain from side to side. If that doesn't work, put the chain on the chain tool in position (B) and turn the handle a little. If that doesn't do it, turn the chain over and push from the other direction.

WORN CHAIN. Chains wear out and stretch. Look where the chain goes around the chainwheel. Pull the chain forward. Does it fit snug or is it loose? A worn chain can cause the chain to slip. If your chain is worn, check both the chainwheel and freewheel sprockets for wear also (see p. 83). Any one alone may be worn, but often all should be replaced.

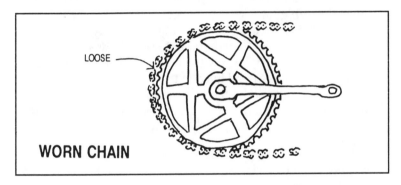

CLEANING AND LUBRICATION. It's a good idea to remove the chain and clean it regularly. To clean the chain well: remove, soak in kerosene, dry thoroughly (let it hang up overnight), then lubricate (with graphite, teflon or silicone-based lubricant although heavy motor oil will work also). You can also lubricate the chain as you turn the pedals with the chain on the bike. Wipe off excess (because excess may collect unwanted dirt).

RIDE CAREFULLY!!!

ANCIENT HISTORY

or HOW THIS BOOK CAME TO BE

This book has such an interesting history that I thought I'd share it.

I've loved bicycles since I was little. I remember a big old-fashioned tricycle, much bigger and more usable than those we have now. I lived in New York City but in an area with places a little kid could safely ride a tricycle. At some point I graduated to a big fat-tired one speed bike and then finally to a three-speed. Then we moved just out of the city limits, to a suburb with no public transportation. My bike was my main transportation —and it was my freedom. I rode it to school and everywhere. My best friend lived in the next town and we spent many hours going to each other's houses and on longer trips. In high school I began going on long day and weekend trips with the American Youth Hostel group in New York.

Then I went off to college in Massachussetts, still using my bike every day to get to classes and for occasional trips around Cambridge and Boston.

In 1967 I came west to San Francisco, where I taught in a parent-teacher run alternative elementary and junior high school for four years (and got a used 10-speed bike which I took on a number of school bike trips). The school was wonderful but had no money to pay teachers so we all scrambled to find other ways to earn enough money to survive.

Through a process much too long to describe here, another teacher, T White, and I decided to open a small bike shop after school. We prospered and soon had a loyal clientele in spite of very limited hours. Maybe it was the teacher in us, but we spent much of our time teaching customers how to fix their own bikes. We let people work in the shop and use our tools. There were no bike repair books at that time and one day I got tired of repeating the same things all the time and decided to write it all down. T White, a former sculptor, illustrated the text.

90

Another friend worked in a print shop and offered to print up some books after hours. He printed 200 copies and we tied them with yarn.

I had just intended the book for our shop but customers liked it and urged me to print it up like a 'real' book. So I began to learn about printing. The first real edition was 3000 copies.

I put some books in the back of my car and took them around to local bike shops and book stores. They liked the book and gave me ideas for marketing it. Bike and book wholesalers picked it up, which in turn spread it to more and more bike shops and bookstores all around the country. Bicycling Magazine and others reviewed it. I used up the first printing fairly quickly and printed more, and more, and more. I revised the book a few times over the years.

That was 1971 — and now it's 1993 and 250,000 books later. I still teach a little, but I have many interests and now spend most of my time writing books and making films (and walking in the woods). I live way up in the Santa Cruz mountains and ride my bike less often now. Last summer, while visiting cousins in France, one cousin loaned me his mountain bike to get around while I was there which allowed me to spend hours riding down small French country roads. And I decided it was time to do yet another revision...

Other books by Helen Garvy:

I Built Myself A House
How To Fix Your BMX Bicycle
Before You Shoot: A Guide to Low-Budget Film Production
The Immune System: Your Magic Doctor
The BINGO Book series

INDEX

ORDER FORM

If you can't find this book in your local bookstore or bike shop, copy this form and we'll be glad to send you one.

Please send me:

_____ HOW TO FIX YOUR BICYCLE ($6 each)

name: _____

address: _____

_____

Please enclose payment for the book(s) plus $1.50 per book for postage and handling.
California residents add sales tax.

Please also send:

_____ HOW TO FIX YOUR BICYCLE ($6 each) to

name: _____

address: _____

_____

Please enclose payment for the book(s) plus $1.50 per book for postage and handling.
California residents add sales tax.

Bulk rates on request.

Mail to: SHIRE PRESS
26873 Hester Creek Road
Los Gatos, CA 95030